# Unwelcome Good News
## Providence in Human Life

Andrew P. Porter

December 5, 2004

PUBLISHERS
*Eugene, Oregon*

Wipf and Stock Publishers
199 W 8th Ave, Suite 3
Eugene, OR 97401

Unwelcome Good News
Providence in Human Life
By Porter, Andrew P.
Copyright©2004 by Porter, Andrew P.
ISBN: 1-59244-938-7
Publication date 10/11/2004

# Contents

| | | |
|---|---|---|
| Acknowledgments | | v |
| Preface | | vii |
| 1 | The Bright Side | 1 |
| | 1.1 A glimmer of hope . . . . . . . . . . . . . . . . . | 1 |
| | 1.2 The Preposterous Idea . . . . . . . . . . . . . | 5 |
| 2 | Trinity | 13 |
| | 2.1 Embarrassed, Frustrated, Panhandled . . . . . . . . | 13 |
| | 2.2 What's a Body to Do? . . . . . . . . . . . . . . . | 18 |
| | 2.3 Three Faces of God . . . . . . . . . . . . . . | 21 |
| | 2.4 On Being Destroyed . . . . . . . . . . . . . . | 23 |
| 3 | Origins | 27 |
| | 3.1 Dumézil . . . . . . . . . . . . . . . . . . . . . | 27 |
| | 3.2 Three-Part Worlds . . . . . . . . . . . . . . . | 30 |
| | 3.3 Inversions . . . . . . . . . . . . . . . . . . . . | 33 |
| 4 | But Why? | 37 |
| | 4.1 Because it's There . . . . . . . . . . . . . . . | 37 |
| | 4.2 That's The Way Things Are . . . . . . . . . . . . | 40 |
| | 4.3 Hidden In Plain Sight . . . . . . . . . . . . . . | 41 |

| | | | |
|---|---|---|---|
| 5 | Who Turned The Lights Out? | | **49** |
| | 5.1 | Panic | 49 |
| | 5.2 | Atheists Who Believe in God | 51 |
| | 5.3 | The Far Side | 57 |
| | 5.4 | Five Easy Pieces | 62 |
| | 5.5 | Unanswerable Questions | 66 |
| | 5.6 | Analogies | 69 |
| | 5.7 | How To Break Anything | 74 |
| | 5.8 | Bag Lady | 78 |
| | 5.9 | I Am Not Making This Up | 81 |
| 6 | Here With Us | | **91** |
| | 6.1 | Children's Games | 91 |
| | 6.2 | Creating the Beginning | 94 |
| | 6.3 | The Three Thing | 99 |
| | 6.4 | What You Mean Three, White Man? | 105 |
| | 6.5 | History, Relativity, and Pluralism | 111 |
| 7 | In The End | | **117** |
| | 7.1 | Against Theodicy | 117 |
| | 7.2 | Sauce For the Goose | 122 |
| | 7.3 | You Are Not Alone | 125 |
| | 7.4 | Clearings | 129 |
| | 7.5 | That's Too Simple | 136 |
| For Further Reading | | | **141** |
| Index | | | **146** |

# Acknowledgments

Those who know will recognize Edward Hobbs' theology on every page. He is not often cited or quoted, because most of his theology was presented in classroom instruction. But the debt is there nonetheless, and I am happy to acknowledge it. If you like this, credit him. If you don't, it's my responsibility. We do have known disagreements, some of which matter greatly, especially in regard to life issues, section 7.4. Still, my debt to my teacher is beyond reckoning.

To my engineering friends, who gave me a hard time, occasionally accusing me of being an atheist, I owe a different kind of debt. They have a certain privacy, and so I shall not name them here, but my gratitude and esteem remain nonetheless. I hope this short book works as at least the beginning of an explanation.

I am indebted to Fr. Gregory Rocca, OP, Fr. Edward Beutner, Mrs. Camille Giglio, and Professors Paul Chung, Edward Hobbs, and James Kraft, for reading all or parts of the manuscript, and to Jonathan Weitsman, for many conversations that lie in the background of these ruminations on hope.

Two lines from John Michael Murphy's sonnet, "Lent," are quoted by permission.

This book was set in Times Roman with TeX and LaTeX macros on a Debian Gnu Linux box.

# Preface

A book such as this is meant to give voice to hope for those who might not otherwise find it. In a word, the possibility that amidst the pains of life there might be some good. That much is clear in the first few pages of the first chapter. If a preface is not needed, that's the place to begin.

What is not so obvious is that for many, this book may not seem to offer hope at all. For in the approach taken here, much that is "traditional" gets questioned, much gets relativized. Much gets vindicated at the cost of being first overthrown, like classical mechanics at the hands of relativity and quantum mechanics in the twentieth century. This is an attempt to make sense of a more or less traditional faith in the light of the challenges of the modern world, but it is impossible to make *traditional* sense of the traditional faith in the modern world. The world has changed in the last three or four centuries, and it strikes me as irresponsible to try to retreat into the imagined past before the modern world. It also seems unnecessary.

This book is hardly a demonstration (let alone a proof) that it is possible to find good in life, despite its manifold pains. But proof that one's faith is justified is not what I had in mind in this book. It is not a derivation but a question, not like Anselm proving the existence of God but like Anselm's faith seeking understanding. It is more than just an inquiry, though; it is also a challenge. It is like the great Deuteronomic sermon in the end of Joshua: Which gods will you serve? What is your pleasure? The inquiry assumes that a choice has already been made, that you want to treat life as good in full view of its pains, and asks how one might live such a life.

In a word, this book is not a theodicy, an argument that this world is good. To claim that the world is good is a confessional commitment, not a derivation, and if one undertakes this commitment, one does so in full view of the pains of life. Nor is this book a defense of God in face of evil: that's what *theodicy* means. To defend God is a futile task: first your client skips bail, then he won't cooperate in his own defense. Worse, there is something very odd about even thinking that God would answer to a human court. The problems only begin there; for to attempt to defend God in face of evil seems usually to end up as defending evil itself, or as leaving the suffering alone in their suffering. On the contrary, this book is an inquiry about how one might live on the basis of taking the world as good. Faith may find resources for meeting the challenge of evil in life—but not in theodicy, as D. Z. Phillips once said (Phillips, 1986, p. 75). Yet faith remains an assumption, a starting point, not the result of a deduction. And one of the first implications is, as John Paul II said in *Salvifici Doloris*, "a singular challenge to communion and solidarity."

This book is written so that rumors of God in his functional presence might not die out. It is written so that those who want to affirm life in full view of its pains and wrongs may do so with recognition and intention. It is incidentally a protest and a reproach against a society that views inescapable pain as not just painful but evil, to be avoided at all costs, because it is thought to be barren, devoid of all blessing.

# Chapter 1

# The Bright Side

## 1.1  A glimmer of hope

Years ago, when I first started taking courses in theology, people used to ask what I was doing. (After finishing a dissertation in computational physics, this was an odd thing to do, and it attracted some puzzlement.) The answer is not entirely obvious, but it comes in the form of another question. What if you wanted to treat all of life as good, in full view of its pains? It is not *simply* that all of life is good, because its pains can clearly be overwhelming. But is it possible to find life good, including its hard and painful parts? It will not always be easy to live that way.

This offered some hope for my questioners, and I think they understood easily that it was about the central challenge of human life: what to do about the pains. Henry David Thoreau once said that most people live lives of quiet desperation. I hope this is not true, but there is certainly a truth in it: People have desires, and often some of their more cherished desires go disappointed. People do not generally get all they want out of life, and eventually, they have to come to terms with the disappointments, with the limitations that they are up against.

Just to put the question baldly, What do you want out of life?
And what if you don't get it?

(What if you *do* get it, and it turns out not to be what you really wanted after all?)

What if *all* of life were good?

Is it even *possible* for *all* of life to be good?

If all of life is good, it would have to be counted good in full view of its hurts, which are many, and plain for all to see.

To some people, it *is* good. That's a risky thing to say, and it puts me out on a limb. Still, that's an interesting place to be. To say that life is good and then quit without more explanation is surely misleading. Quite possibly it sounds like it's coming from someone who has been exempted from major pains. But those who believe all of life is good get rained on just as much as those who don't. They are destroyed in the end, just like everybody else is. Having lived long enough to watch a few other people for a fair fraction of their lives, it is clear to me that people's hopes and expectations are all too often betrayed in the middle of life; we do not get what we thought we wanted.

To say that life, including its pains, is good is not the same thing as saying that it all has meaning. To find good in the pains of life is often to trust when we cannot see any meaning in them, even to trust as we are being destroyed. And it does not help to say that God knows the meaning of the pains of our lives as we could know (if only we did). Always, the warning in Isaiah 55.8 is to be remembered: "my thoughts are not your thoughts, my ways are not your ways." It is dangerous to think of God in human terms—doing that can all too easily turn God into a monster. Sometimes we can see the good in the pains of life, sometimes we cannot. Always we can trust.

One more thing should be seen in passing; it is the larger context, or perspective in which life is viewed, and that is *history*: Man is not only like other creatures in nature, who are *just* part of nature. Though man comes from nature, he has a *history*, and without understanding history and locating man in history, it is impossible to make sense of human life. Nature is part of history, but history goes well beyond what can be explained as "just natural." I shall have relatively little to

## 1.1 A glimmer of hope

say about history in this book, in order to keep things to a manageable size and to focus on one central idea. (Nevertheless, chapters 3 and 6 are essentially historical in their logic.) It should not be forgotten that history stands in the background in an indispensable way. History will appear in the lead role in other books, as it did in *By the Waters of Naturalism*. Indeed, there is much that is not here. What is here is little more than the basic affirmation of life in this world.

So let's see what it means to say that life is good, all of it, including its pains. The pains of life are the test of any attitude toward life. That is why we begin with them.

Perhaps the best way to begin is just to tell the story of how the beans got spilled. When I finished a thesis doing physics on a computer, after many months of sustained work late at night into wee hours, on a computer that filled a large room, going spacey with air-conditioning noise, I needed a break. So I signed up to take a first-year course in critical tools, basic texts, and the historical background for the Bible. It was the general introduction for divinity students, but it has a broader appeal than just for those preparing for ordination. Edward Hobbs and Donn Morgan taught it. Hobbs is a New Testament scholar, Morgan an Old Testament scholar. The course was wild beyond even my rather wild dreams, and most of what it covered can't be told in this book, because there isn't room. The Bible is a mixed collection, and even individual books were put together in ways that can now be reconstructed with fair confidence, giving us a history that quite exceeds the common ideas about it.

One day the inevitable question got asked in class. Someone wanted to know about miracles. I think that Edward Hobbs was talking about the difference between the probable and the merely possible, and about how a historian is stuck with what is probable. Maybe he mentioned Ernst Troeltsch, a German philosopher of history who upset theologians in a big way back at the turn of the century. (The turn of the last century, 1900, not 2000!) We were not ready for Troeltsch yet, and Troeltsch is not part of my story in this book. (He got a brief mention in *Waters*.) In any case, Troeltsch spoke for the historical skeptics, and after Troeltsch many things look different. What was thought to be central (the "miracles," in their literal interpretation) were gone. What had been noticed but generally ignored now appeared front and center: the Exodus. Thereby hangs a tale for another time. (Some of it was in *Waters*.)

But what Edward Hobbs *did* say in answer to the question about miracles was life-changing. He said that the difference between Israelite religion and the religion of the surrounding Canaanite tribes was not that the God of Israel produced real miracles and the other gods, the Baals and the Ashtartes, produced fake miracles or none at all. To the extent that any of those peoples believed in "miracles," they all did, Israelites no less than and no differently from the Canaanites, Egyptians, Syrians, Hittites, Babylonians, and so on. They all shared a common world-view, a common view of what sort of things happen and what sort of things don't happen, what's possible and what's not.

The difference between biblical religion and the surrounding "pagan" religions was quite other than anything to do with miracles. (I shall have a much more complimentary term for the pagan religions than the word "pagan," but it will take some time to get to it. Some people today consider the word "pagan" itself to be complimentary enough, and they have revived it for their own use.) The difference between Israelite religion and Canaanite religion was that for Israelite religion, the God brings good in all of life, in the pains just as much as the pleasures. For Canaanite religion, when the pains come, it means that your gods are either powerless or else seriously ticked off. Time to bargain with them, or to get better ones. Moderns might say that broken gods should be fixed or traded in. When the gods are angry, you bargain, bribe, plead, or placate. When the gods are powerless, other measures are necessary. If you have been conquered, perhaps you just adopt the gods of the conquerors. But you do whatever it takes to get rid of the pains of life and get the pleasures back, because the pains are barren, the pains don't bring any good at all.

It was otherwise with Israelite religion. For the Hebrews, as they were when things got started, if the God brings pains in life, it is because he has some blessing intended within the pains. This was not particularly easy, and they doubted a lot, and complained a lot, but the essential idea was there at the beginning, and it has been the seed for biblical religion ever since. In the words of Karl Barth's *Commentary on the Epistle to the Romans*, when life says No to you, it is because within that No, God is saying a Yes to you. It may not be one that is obvious, but it is there nonetheless.

## 1.2 The Preposterous Idea

So what does it mean to choose to treat all of life as good, hard and painful parts included?

First, it is not the position of Leibniz, satirized by Voltaire in *Candide*, that this world is the best of all possible worlds. You could easily specify a world more to your liking, and so could anyone. Voltaire's answer to chatter about the best of all possible worlds is not bad: shut up and pull weeds. But if, as a matter of choice, and in full view of all the pains of life, you wanted to treat human life in this world as good, as blessed, not worrying about whether this world is the best of all possible worlds or not, how would it work? To say that it is a matter of choice does not quite capture the meaning of the choice. For if it is *just* a choice, then it has no implications for other people. But even though it is a choice, we shall eventually see that it really does have implications for other people. For to live one way instead of another is to claim, implicitly, that the one way is better than the other.

The pains are not good because they are painful, they are good because they are part of life. The pain is incidental; the events themselves are what is good. It is always right to complain about the pain, to admit honestly that it hurts. It is quite another matter to take offense *at life* because of the pains—or at "God," if the idea of "God" makes sense. One may and should take offense at human wrongdoing, but life itself? That is another matter. If life is good, then all its parts are in some sense good, hurt though they may. At least that is the preposterous idea of radical monotheism.

There are plenty of biblical examples, starting in the first chapter of Genesis. For that creation story is a parody of cosmogonies from the surrounding cultures (and a much abbreviated one). In the surrounding cultures, the beginning of the world is a contest between good and evil, order and chaos, and it is not at all obvious that the good will win. It takes a struggle, and the evil to some extent remains to challenge the good in life ever after. Those surrounding cultures did affirm the world as good, in a limited and qualified sense. They did not repudiate the world as evil and defective, as Gnostics later did. (The Gnostics are well beyond our story in this little book.) Much as they may have wanted to affirm human life in this world as good, the Canaanites and Babylonians and Egyptians had trouble integrating *all* of life into that good.

In Genesis 1, by contrast, God pronounces the world and everything in it good no less than seven times. There is no evil opposition, no struggle. Trouble does not appear until human beings eat of the tree of "knowledge of good and evil," i.e., until human beings start making distinctions between good and evil. ("Knowing" here is very active; it means a way of relating to the world, not just knowing how the world is, independently of human knowers.)

Later on, Abraham is given a commission, to be a blessing to all peoples (Genesis 12), and with that commission, a promise, that he will have lots of children. In an age when conception was iffy, when childbirth was dangerous, when children often did not survive infancy, this was a promise of no mean significance. To have lots of children was to prosper. It was (literally!) to have life more abundantly. That is the promise—life more abundantly.

When Moses asks God who He is, before returning from the burning bush to his friends in Egypt, Moses speaks for their cares. God merely assures Moses that He will be "with them"—thus touching the

## 1.2 The Preposterous Idea    7

nerve of their anxieties. Will we be left alone? The promise of the Bible is that no, despite our apparent aloneness, we are not abandoned.

When Solomon turns out to be a despot (read the beginning of 1 Kings, chapters 1-2 and 12; most people don't know these passages), the Abraham covenant is brought back to mind to hold Solomon and his sons to account. To be a blessing to all peoples indeed! A rare injunction to justice, fairness, and generosity.

When things look darkest, when the Assyrians have long ago carried off little Israel into oblivion, when the Babylonians are doing the same to little Judah, what happens? The parts of the Bible that come from that period tells us. Job poses the problem of affliction, and Isaiah escalates the problem. Isaiah 40-54 is known as Deutero-Isaiah, because it is clearly from an author later than the one who started the book. Within Deutero-Isaiah there are four poems known as the "Servant Songs," because they are about the Servant of the Lord. They were not written about Jesus, though Christians later used them to make sense of Jesus. You are familiar with the fourth of those songs, from Handel's Messiah; it is a musical version of Isaiah 52-53. ("Surely, he hath borne our griefs, and carried our sorrows: yet we did esteem him stricken, smitten of God, and afflicted.") The servant is a young man, handsome and graceful, and he suffers for others. How can good come out of suffering? Why should one person suffer for another? And what on earth possessed God to use one person's afflictions to set things right with other people?

The problem of suffering is not just in the Servant Songs. Isaiah 45.7 (Jerusalem Bible, altered) focuses it:

> I am the LORD, unrivalled,
> I form the light and create the dark,
>
> I make good fortune and create calamity,
> it is I, the LORD, who do all this.

It is of course possible to twist this passage, to interpret it in more than one way. For the pains of life could be intended only for the wicked, and the pleasures as rewards for the good. But I don't think that's what Isaiah had in mind here, for these words are addressed to the good, to the faithful but faint of heart, to strengthen them. The pains come to the just and the unjust alike. And the just suffer. Isaiah had something positive in mind here, but what? Job picks it up (whether before or after the verse in Isaiah is not known with certainty) and asks (2.10), "If we take happiness from God's hand, must we not take sorrow too?"

The New Testament picks it up in the narrative of the Gospels (in a way, they are modeled on the Suffering Servant), but the New Testament is usually not very theoretical about it. Romans 8.28 is an exception, for Paul there says that "all things work together for good for them that love God." Paul labors around the problem of the pains of life in chapter 8, confident that good will be brought out of them sooner or later. We shall have more to say about the Gospels momentarily. They deal with the problem in narrative, not in doctrine or philosophy.

Isaiah 45.7 gets picked up in the Siddur,

> Blessed art thou, O Lord our God, King of the Universe, who formest light and createst darkness, who makes peace and createst all things.

The text is discreet: where it has "all things," Isaiah has "evil." The rabbis' discretion is appropriate, in respect for the magnitude of suffering in the world, but the source is obvious to all who know the Bible. This blessing is central to Jewish daily prayer, announced every morning in the blessings before the Shema. I am indebted to Jonathan Weitsman for this passage, in many conversations, over many years.

In the Talmud, things are clearer. The Babylonian Talmud is a collection whose oldest parts overlap the last documents in the New Testament. The Mishnah, the core of the Talmud, was published about the time the New Testament canon was closed, around 200 CE. It was finished some centuries later, as legends and commentary on the Mishnah were added. (Where the New Testament makes its points

## 1.2 The Preposterous Idea

indirectly, in stories that the reader may or may not get, the Talmud can be like an American students' dream—an instruction manual, plain, to the point, do this, don't do that. But the Talmud can also be even more baffling than the New Testament.)

Berakhot is one of the tractates in the Talmud, a small book in itself. It is about blessings (that's what its name means), when to say them, how to say them, what to say them for, and so on. Chapter 9 of the tractate has a lot in it, in one way or another, about good and evil. Not exactly in the same tone as Romans 8, but there are uncanny resonances. At one point in it, the rabbis are perplexed. They ask themselves whether Mishnah Berakhot 9.5 can really mean what it says: "A man is obliged to recite a blessing over evil just as he recites a blessing over good." (Jacob Neusner's translation, p. 14.) The Mishnah continues, interestingly enough, with a quotation of the Shema, "You shall love the Lord with all your heart, with all your soul, and with all your might," by way of justification for the injunction to bless for evil as for good. Few passages could be more central to the character and meaning of the God of the Bible than this one.

As the rabbis puzzle their way through this text in the Mishnah, we hear, "one must accept [evil] with gladness"; "The Lord gave and the Lord has taken away, blessed be the name of the Lord (Job 1:21)"; "Whatever the All-Merciful does is for the good." (Neusner's translation, p. 408; Bavli, folio 60b.) They are pretty clear about it. The text behind this is Isaiah 45.7, which we have seen already.

What I have left out of this catalog of texts (other than the Gospels, with which we begin in the next chapter) is the Exodus. You could say that this kind of religion is a world-affirming historical religion, and in this book, we only look at the "world-affirming" part. Exodus, by contrast, is about the historical part of this religion as the origin of its world-affirming part. Its intense focus on history will have to wait for another time. But it is there, at the beginning of the story in the Bible, even if I don't begin with it here in this book.

World-affirming historical religions are to be contrasted with world-affirming nature religions, religions that have no interest in history, and seek instead to affirm human life in the world on the assumption that nature is all there is. ("World-affirming nature religion" is a functional description of "pagan" religion, and one that is much less polemical today.) The Canaanite and Egyptian and Babylonian religions were of this type, and the Hebrews borrowed heavily from them all. The world-affirming part, however, was very qualified in the nature religions. Israelite religion radicalized it.

What's at stake is the doctrine of creation, for what creation *means* is that the world is good. To be *created* means to be declared good. The Hebrew words for create (*bara*) and bless (*berakoth*) are not from the same root, and so not related, but the ideas tend to appear together in the Common Documents. (I shall call the documents shared in the Jewish and Christian Bibles the Common Documents, because they are the documents shared in common by the Church and the Synagogue. This term is both accurate and also the least prejudicial of the terms I know for this literature.) In modern thinking, *create* just means *make*, in the sense of physically causing something to be or to happen. That meaning is secondary. To bless means to wish someone well. It is not just about having enough food, it means someone else wants you to be happy.

So the preposterous starting point is that when life says No, then deep down, it means Yes. Let's look at how that happens, in chapter 2. There we shall see a particular three-part pattern of pains and remedies, disappointments and blessings. In chapter 3, we shall see the cultural origins of that three-part pattern, and also the characteristic inversion of radical monotheism in which the disappointments and pains of life are transformed to bring blessing. In chapter 4, we ask why one should look at life this way; after all, it hurts, and a few reasons would be comforting. There are none. At that point, you might begin to feel somewhat alone and abandoned, and chapter 5 will look at that state of aloneness. It's called transcendence. When we look for transcendence, if we do not deceive ourselves, and if we know what we are looking

*1.2 The Preposterous Idea* 11

for, we are gently turned around, back to this world. When we return to this world, what we come to are the origins of this faith in history. That's chapter 6. Chapter 7 will look at some cautions and a few applications.

# Chapter 2

# Trinity

## 2.1 Embarrassed, Frustrated, Panhandled

Things get a little clearer if we have some concrete examples. If all of life is good, taken as an article of faith, what do you do about the hard parts? Much of life hurts, and in the end, I shall be destroyed. You can draw your own conclusions about what will happen to you.

Well, what kind of hard parts did you have in mind? Look at three kinds that are different enough so that none of them can just be turned into cases of the others. In the acknowledgements at the start of the book, I said that most of what's here follows Edward Hobbs's earlier work. That is especially true in this chapter, for what follows is pretty much a student's memory of Professor Hobbs's classroom teaching, if presented in the student's words.

First, the situation of being caught red-handed, embarrassed, *exposed*. You may be guilty, you may be innocent, everybody may be confused, but you didn't want to be seen this way in public. That's one kind of disappointment. Exposure affects how you look, how legitimate you appear to be.

Second, frustration, when you wanted to do something but couldn't (or didn't want to, and were ordered or forced to). Frustration is a kind of *limitation*, and it affects your ability to act.

Third are times when other people ask you for help, help when you had other plans. They want your time, your effort, your resources. You have been panhandled, sponged upon, shaken down, imposed upon. Other people's *needs* affect your resources, your food supply, and so on.

When Edward Hobbs explained radical monotheism to his students, exposure, limitation, and need were what he talked about. You can find variations on them in many Christian writers. This is not a particularly Jewish way of *cataloging* the disappointments of life, as we shall see in coming sections, when we look at how to expand this series. The Gospel responses are, nevertheless, a very Jewish way of *responding* to the disappointments of life. The Evangelists wrote in Greek, which will account for the three-part organization. Jesus was thoroughly Jewish, which explains his covenantal openness to the work of God as it comes in the pains of life. These three disappointments don't appear as a series in the Common Documents, though you can certainly find them all there in one place or another. That, after all, is where Jesus got his ideas. We have seen it in Romans 8, where Paul wrestles with the pains of life in the light of a confidence that comes, among other places, from Isaiah 45, from Job, and from the Servant Songs in Isaiah 40-55.

Exposure does appear in the New Testament, in many places, but especially in the Gospels. For Mark (the earliest of the Gospels) barely begins when the teaching of Jesus starts, in 1.15: the time has come, the kingdom of God is upon you, it's time to repent! In other words, the jig is up, you'd better repent while you can. Matthew 4.33 has about the same words. We meet exposure early, and the message is to embrace it. We'll soon see what you get when you embrace it.

In another story, this one in Matthew, the parable of the laborers in the vineyard, Jesus takes people to task for being envious. The owner hires people every three hours, from seven in the morning until five in the afternoon, and an hour later, he pays them all the same wage.

## 2.1 Embarrassed, Frustrated, Panhandled 15

Those who worked through the day are hot, tired, thirsty, and envious. Jesus says to quit making invidious comparisons between yourself and your neighbor, and accept life in gratitude and joy. Luke 12.22, makes much the same point in another way, about trust in providence: "If the smallest things, therefore, are out of your control, why worry about the rest?" Matthew 6.25 ff. has the same story.

Lastly, Jesus often enough enjoins people to help those in need. Luke 12.33: sell all you have and give alms. Or the parable of the Good Samaritan, a story of many messages, but help for others in need large among them. Or Matthew 25.31 ff., "when you did it to the least of these, you did it to me:" "For I was hungry and you gave me food, I was thirsty and you gave me drink, ... sick and you visited me, in prison and you came to see me." There's not much in the teaching that cannot be fitted into one or another of the general commands to repent, to accept life in joy and gratitude, and to help others in need.

What about the miracles? Jesus cleanses, raises, and feeds people. It may seem odd to break the healings up into cleansings and raisings, and cleansing is perhaps the oddest of the three. Lest there be any doubt, the word for cleansing, *katharizo*, sometimes gets repeated three times in one story. What does not go without saying is the background, and that background is in Leviticus, a good part of which is about the clean and the unclean. Every Jew would have known it, and would have understood what it means to be unclean and need cleansing. Skin diseases are the most obvious case of uncleanness, but unclean spirits are implied by extension, too. What is strange to us is that cleansing is a form of healing from moral uncleanness as well as physical uncleanness. Here we see exposure as a form of healing. More to the point, perhaps, at least for us, is the little sentence or two at the beginning of many of the healings, in which the one about to be healed first receives forgiveness of sins. The crowd often doubted whether forgiveness was even possible, and the idea that forgiveness is freely given to any who want it still seems a little loose, too easy, even today. The unclean spirits are encountered in a way that is very exposing for the patient, the one possessed: his, after all, is the mouth that the unclean spirit speaks through, his is the mouth that defies Jesus, and his is the body that is exhausted after it is all over. And he is the one who is freed—newly able to go about his life without the burden of the past.

So we see the problem of sin dealt with aplenty, in healing exposure. What about limitation? The Greek word for raising, *egeiro*, is used more often than one might think from the translations. In Mark 3.1, the story of the man with the withered hand, the English translators almost never get it right. In French, where there is a common French idiom ready to hand, they did: Lève-toi là, au milieu! Raise yourself up here in the center! Usually, *egeiro* gets translated by convenient words, and the emphasis it gives doesn't show through clearly in the English. Raising the dead, raising the sick. At the end, of course, is the biggest raising of all, the Resurrection.

Sickness is a form of limitation. When you're sick, you can't do what you wanted to do. When you're paralyzed, you can't walk. In one episode (Mark 2.1), Jesus is preaching to a crowd inside a house. A paralyzed man has four friends bring him to be healed, but they can't get in. They climb up on the roof, and dig a hole in the roof, and lower him down on a body-bag (that's what the Greek word, *krabbaton*, means) just as if they were burying him. Jesus raises him, after first forgiving his sins.

The feedings are a fairly clear case of taking care of need. There are three of them in the Synoptic Gospels, one with five loaves left over, one with seven loaves left over; and a thirteenth loaf later in the bottom of the boat with the disciples, just a bit too conspicuously inconspicuous. A few loaves and a few fish feed them all.

Preposterous—and deliberately so! For all of these "miracles" are impossible, and we are supposed to know that they are impossible. They are like TV advertisements, where the preposterous regularly happens, but with a difference: These are more like Saturday Night Live or Monty Python doing *parodies* of TV ads. We know that the

## 2.1 Embarrassed, Frustrated, Panhandled

sick are not healed this casually, we know that food does not stretch this far. So what is the product, in these mock-advertisements? These people live with exposure, limitation, and need, and they go away happy. How does it happen?

Now you may complain, that I don't believe in "miracles" ("TV Ads," in *Waters*) or that I am trashing the point of the miracle stories ('Happy Easter," in *Waters*?). What *is* the point of the miracle stories? That Jesus will help you get out of the disappointments of life? That the model of the miracle stories is meant to encourage you *not* to embrace exposure when it comes? Exposure doesn't help? The truth does *not* do you any good when it hurts? And so also for limitation and need? What, after all, was the point of the teaching to repent, if Jesus is going to exempt you from exposure, prevent embarrassment from coming to you? What, after all, was the point of the teaching about accepting your life and its limitations in gratitude and joy, if Jesus is going to get you out of those limitations? What, after all, was the point about helping others, if the feeding stories are telling us that bread grows on trees?

Truly, if you think that exposure, limitation, and need are barren, and you just want to avoid them, you may get what you ask for—but it won't be what Jesus is offering. In Mark, the disciples are a little slow, they think Jesus is going to give them power and control: precisely exemption *from* the pains of life, not blessing *in* life—including its pains. Jesus eventually has to remind them of what he has been saying all along: Repent, the jig is up; accept life in gratitude and joy, not invidious comparisons between yourself and your neighbor; and help your neighbor in need. If the miracles are about getting *out* of the pains of life, they hardly make sense if he has been telling people to find blessings *in* exposure, limitation, and need. But the miracle stories *do* make sense if we take them ironically—in full knowledge that "miraculous" healings don't "literally" happen. It is a joyful irony, to be sure, and not a bitter one, but an irony just the same.

We see the same things in the Common Documents, if not in this peculiar three-part organization. The texts are full of injunctions to help your neighbor in need, and it is not necessary to catalog them. (That would take a long time; there are many passages!) That they show us people embracing exposure is only a little less obvious. When David arranges that Bathsheba's husband Uriah will die in combat, and then takes Bathsheba to wife, he is confronted by Nathan the prophet. David repents and acknowledges his wrongdoing. But this picturesque story is only a banner-passage for what is everywhere. For the prophets over and over again say that when disasters comes, as it will, it will bring truth with it, exposure of apostasy from the covenant. And as for limitation, look at the very name of the people that the Hebrews became: Israel, the new name of one of their forebears, Jacob. Jacob was renamed Israel (twice), and the name Isra-el means the one who struggles with God. That is to say, one who struggles with limitation, and in it finds blessing. Jacob makes an interesting contrast to the mythical figure of Prometheus, for both struggle with limitation. But Israel struggles in faith and ultimately in trust and in gratitude. Prometheus struggles in rebellion, distrust, defiance, resentment, and offense.

## 2.2 What's a Body to Do?

How, then, does one find the blessing in the pains of life? Differently in each of the three cases, but the responses are very much in the same spirit.

To exposure of how you really are, contrary to how you wanted to appear, you respond with acknowledgement of the truth. What is exposed may or may not be wrong. (Unwelcome exposure can come when what is exposed is innocent, and then the responses will be a little different from those to exposure of sin.) Assume for the moment that what is exposed is wrongful. The first response is to acknowledge the truth, to confess, to come clean. After acknowledgement comes repentance, a kind of "turning around" of the mind and of the will. Then

## 2.2 What's a Body to Do?

comes remorse, a sadness, emotional pain at what one has become. Lastly, though, when the matter has been worked through, there comes real freedom, for you are now no longer bound to the past. You may be bound to *pay* for the past, but you are not bound to try to *cover up* the past. You are no longer stuck trying to continue a form of life that was wrong.

To limitation, the responses are similar. You accept the limitations as they are, and are willing to work with them. When limitation is painful, there is a natural grief. But in the end, there is gratitude, celebration. What comes out of it all is creativity, the ability to do something with the limitation. When the limitation is terminal (immanent death), often all that one can do is give a blessing to those close by. But that is enough. In the end, there is gratitude and celebration.

How do you respond to another in need? An unwelcome other in need? By opening your eyes, your hands, and your heart, to help. In the end, there comes real fellowship, community, and once again, celebration.

Let me return to the exception noted above, for exposure, when what is exposed is innocent. What exactly is the sort of exposure that discloses more or less innocent human existence but is nevertheless unwelcome? The sort of cases that I can imagine all have a common thread in them. We wish that we were in control, we wish that we were able to dispose of our lives. And we are revealed not to be in control but to be vulnerable, to be mistaken about the real situation of our lives, to be a product of circumstances that came before us when we thought we had made ourselves. There is a technical term for human life lived under these conditions. It is called being a "creature," someone who is not in control. The response parallels confession, and so on—but here it just takes the form of laughter! Acknowledge the true situation, laugh, and move on. The Far Side cartoon series was particularly good at showing us people in their creaturehood. People loved it because it was true—and they could laugh. We shall come back to it, in section 5.3.

Do you always know what the true limitations are? Of course not. You often have to struggle to find out what the limitations are. That's why Jacob was renamed Israel, the one who Struggles With God. The real possibilities where you find yourself today are often not at all obvious. And realizing those possibilities requires first a guess as to what they are, and second a lot of effort to make them actually happen. If you are a wife and your husband is beating you, does that mean you have to submit? Certainly not! What *is* the limitation here? The limitation, for the wife, is the husband's bad character. How to deal with it is open. Encouraging violence by submitting to violence when other options are possible (calling the police) is hardly a very creative way of dealing with limitation.

Does the other person always have a claim on you when he says "I am in need, so please hand over all your money"? Sometimes. Sometimes he really is in need. Sometimes this is just a shakedown.

There is a certain judgement required. But the *spirit* of response is still supposed to be generous and open, which is why Jesus's stories about it are so preposterous. When people ask "how much am I supposed to give?," he always says "all you have," but when Zacchaeus offers to give half, Jesus laughs and says "Awright-awready, enough, enough!" (Then they party.)

And it is not as if exposure is always unwelcome; or limitation or need, for that matter. Some limitations are foreseen and welcomed without any experience of pain, you know they are coming, you are prepared, you know what to do, and creativity is easy on the emotions, even when it costs a lot of effort. Sometimes limitation is welcomed even *with* its pains, as in athletic training. The same goes for the encounters with need and exposure. If you choose to embrace all of life, its pains included, we can tell pretty clearly what lies in store for you when you embrace exposure, limitation, and need.

If you embrace exposure, if you admit the truth about yourself, you may have to make some changes in your life. But you will get freedom, freedom from hiding the past, freedom from the burden of the past. Your concealment will turn to remorse and then to relief.

If you embrace limitation, and accept it, you will find the opportunities that lie in it. (This is called creativity.) Your grief will turn to gratitude.

If you embrace your neighbor's need, with open hands, open eyes, and open heart, you will get community. Your loneliness will turn to fellowship and celebration.

If you reject exposure, limitation, and need? In the end, you will get falseness, stubbornness, and hard-heartedness. But mostly, in the meantime, you will succeed in covering it all up and looking respectable. What's your pleasure? Choose.

## 2.3 Three Faces of God

These responses to the pains of life have a larger role in the Christian life than one might at first suspect from this brief description of them. For in each one, you meet one Person of the Trinity. Exposure is about sin, right and wrong, and redemption from sin comes from God the Son. Setting people free from their sins is the primary work of the Son. In limitation, you meet the contingencies of creation, the facts of life, the world as it is rather than as you would like it to be. In other words, you meet God the Father, the creator. In other people's need, you stand in the doorway to fellowship, and fellowship is a gift of the Holy Spirit. Things can become somewhat more complicated than this, as we shall see, but this is the simplest and most useful explanation.

The classic statement of it in recent theology is somewhat obscure, in an essay by Edward Hobbs (1970, pp. 32-33). It may be summarized briefly and functionally, without its biblical roots. We respond positively to exposure, to getting caught, when other people can see us as we are, because that exposure brings freedom from the past. We respond positively to limitation, because in limitation we meet our creaturehood and encounter the creator as a loving father whose gifts are not what we expected or wanted but are good nonetheless, often better than what was asked for. This we trust we shall find out in time. We respond positively to others in need, and we benefit from the community that is created as much as they do. In exposure, we meet God the Son, the redeemer from sin; in limitation, we meet God the Father, who blesses us in those very limitations; in others' need, we meet God the Holy Spirit, who brings fellowship, community, and all the sustenance that can only come through other people.

This is an account of the Trinity as it is experienced by human beings, not as it is in itself—or as God is in himself. The usual language speaks of one God in three Persons, but the Greek word that gets translated as "person," *prosopon*, really does not mean what the English word "person" means. Mask would be a better translation for *prosopon*, for the word *prosopon* in one of its original meanings was just the mask that a dramatic actor wore. The Latin translation of *prosopon*, *per-sona*, means "through-sound," i.e., the mask through which the sound of the actor's voice comes. In other words, "mask" here means "role," also a well-attested meaning for *prosopon*. And if mask means role, then one God in three masks means one actor playing three roles. One actor playing three roles—*simultaneously*, all on stage at the same time.

You may protest that one actor can't be on stage in three roles *simultaneously*. But one actor can! Hollywood does it easily whenever the plot of a movie requires it, and if Hollywood can do it, then surely God can, too. Simultaneously is important, for without it, we would have one of the sequential theories of human history in which we move from the age of God the Father to that of God the Son, and soon we'll be in the age of God the Holy Spirit. A recurring theme among fringe groups, but not mainstream Christianity.

What it amounts to is that we see the effects of divine action in our lives, but we do not see God in himself, as he is in himself. (I don't know what it would even *mean* to know God as he is in himself.) But we are shown all that we need to see, if perhaps not all that we would like to see.

This may be uncomfortable. But what people really want, when they want to know God as he is in himself, I think, is to know something that they can get some control over, even if it is only conceptual control. They want something that they can use as proof, or as evidence, something tangible. We shall return to this craving again and again, but for now it is enough to notice it. The God that is known in these three phenomena or in these three masks is with us, even when he cannot be seen. It is important to respect that "cannot be seen."

## 2.4  On Being Destroyed

For those who doubt, there are some questions. Does the truth do you any good when the truth hurts? People usually answer with a Yes—hesitant, but still a yes. Is it really so? Are there times when the truth is too painful to do you any good? When would rejecting the truth really be the better course? When would stonewalling the truth offer more freedom than accepting it? Often the truth can be very costly—but real freedom can often be very costly.

There is a story that Albert Camus told more than once, and it was probably not original with him. In all likelihood, he found it in a newspaper clipping, which is what he makes happen to one of his characters. In the story, there is a family in a remote and mountainous district, someplace out of the mainstream of modern culture. A father, mother, son, daughter. They are innkeepers. The father dies, and the young son realizes that he can't contribute much. Rather than be a drag on his mother and sister, still innkeepers in dire poverty, he goes off to the big city to grow up and earn a living. Meanwhile, the mother and daughter are barely surviving. When single guests come to the inn who look like they will not be missed, they quietly dispose of them and pocket the possessions of the travelers. The son returns, full-grown, and with a beard. They do not recognize him. He checks in, and does not disclose who he is, planning to surprise them in the morning. They do as they usually do, and bury his body out in back. Then, returning to his room, they open his bags and find not only the gold that he must have intended for them, but also tattered photographs of themselves that he has clearly treasured for many years.

In the longer version of the story, one commits suicide and the other goes crazy. This is out of respect for the devastating impact of the exposure. More often than not, people in this situation would reject the truth.

Yet people do embrace exposure: I watched a convicted murderer, interviewed on TV, as his execution approached. He was asked whether people should pity or pray for him. He answered, "No; pray for the people that I killed." David Edwin Mason was executed in the San Quentin gas chamber 1993/08/24, after he withdrew all appeals from the California and Federal courts. (The particulars of the case are in the opinion of the California Supreme Court, "The People v. David Edwin Mason," 52 Cal 3rd. 909; No. S004604, Crim. No. 23519, Jan 10, 1991. The victims were Joan Picard, Arthur Jennings, Antoinette Brown, Dorothy Lang, and Boyd Johnson.) These things do happen, and without invoking anything naturally or socially impossible, they are miraculous: they show forth the grace that comes with embracing exposure. It is not a coincidence that usually, in the New Testament healing miracles, the healed one is first invited to repentance and forgiveness of sin. David Mason died a free man; the mother and daughter in Camus' fictional story did not.

As for exposure, so for limitation, but in a slightly different form. For the question here is one of whether you will take offense at the limitations of life, take offense at something that is hard to specify, but is definitely beyond the particulars of the other people involved. The other people may have wronged you, but the blame extends beyond them, but to what? To life itself? In a way, yes.

Can limitation destroy people? Other than literally, which it always does, in the end? Yes: limitation can destroy people. People live with constraints on what they would like to be and do, and they can be embittered by those constraints in ways that sour their whole lives.

## 2.4 On Being Destroyed

Constraint only appears to be a limitation at all in view of what is available to other people, or at least only by comparison with what you would have wanted. And so just as exposure always involves other people, so also limitation involves other people. Indeed, limitation often is imposed precisely by the will of other people. Our first and last experiences of limitation are in what other people tell us to do or not do.

One always grieves when life hurts; not to would be psychologically dishonest and self-destructive. There is often also a certain natural anger that must be worked through. But taking offense is different, for taking offense at the limitations of life is a way of shutting oneself off from them, closing oneself off to the possibilities in them. One who remains open, on the other hand, is willing to work with the limitations as they come. It is an uncanny coincidence that one of the literal meanings of the German word for "resoluteness," Entschlossenheit, is un-closedness, or just openness. I am told that the meaning of openness has often evaporated from the word, but still, it is interesting that the word for courage means openness to the possibilities that life offers.

Can other people's need destroy? Yes, of course. One can be destroyed by others' need in several ways. The cost in resources and effort may be devastating, and one reacts in bitterness and resentment, even rancor. Or one just stiffs the others in need, and this time, a hardness of heart sets in.

What happens to you depends on how you respond to the pains.

But you can see already that there are plenty of reasons to reject the pains as barren, and many do. Everybody does, at least some of the time.

# Chapter 3

# Origins

## 3.1 Dumézil

When Judaism moved out into the Greek-speaking world, it began to think in terms of a three-part conceptual organization of the world. Even Philo of Alexandria does this. He was a Greek-speaking Jew in the first century CE who wrote to harmonize the Bible and Plato where possible, and prove the superiority of the Bible by showing that Plato got his ideas *from* the Bible. Never mind the fact that Philo was wrong in these claims; he is a perfect example of Jewish thinking in Alexandria at the time. He has no knowledge of or interest in Jesus, though he lived after Jesus by a little bit. In Philo's world, Greek-speaking Judaism of Alexandria, the world usually fits comfortable into three departments. We shall see these three departments in detail as this chapter unfolds, and return to them again in chapter 6. Actually, the anthropologists and linguists call them not departments but *functions*, because in each one of them, something different gets done, and the word for getting something done is just "function." Three-part thinking is not deliberate and intentional and elaborate, as it is in India, but it appears quietly nonetheless. The first of the three functions of life is about legitimacy and order, right and wrong, making sense of things, truth and knowledge. The second function is about force and action, making decisions, getting things done. The third function is about nutrition and sustenance, health, emotions, and fertility.

In the Trinity that we saw in the last chapter, one Person or *prosopon* of the God works in each function. What is odd, though, is that God always fixes what's broken in each department of life, and he does it in a way that helps those who are in trouble in each department or function. God the Son takes care of problems with legitimacy and order—that is, he helps those who are caught in a state of sin. This was exposure. God the Father takes care of those who are up against limitations. In the end, the limitations work to bring blessing. God the Holy Spirit takes care of need, and brings fellowship when you are met by need. This we have seen, odd as it is. We have not seen quite *how* odd it is, and we have not seen the cultural roots of this three-fold organization of life.

There are reasons why biblical religion in the Greek-speaking world should think in terms of these three departments or functions. If those roots can be found, we might understand how we came to think the way we do. Understanding how we came to think like this will tell us how some parts of our thinking are culturally relative; while this does not thereby make them false or wrong, it does put them in an entirely new light.

Christian thinking has always had a tripartite character. Recent research indicates that it is peculiar to cultures speaking Indo-European languages. It is the doctrine of the Trinity which is the most prominent manifestation of this tripartite thinking. The idea of the Trinity was worked out only in the first centuries of the life of the Church, when Christianity moved out into the world of Greek and Roman culture and Indo-European languages. There are certainly roots of the Trinity in the Common Documents, but not the idea itself. Indeed, the idea itself is barely to be found in the New Testament, or so it appears on the surface.

The Indo-European way of thinking seems to be that all human and

## 3.1 Dumézil

divine society is divided in three parts. Indeed, anything interesting at all is divided in three parts. They are the three functions or departments that we saw a moment ago. In the habitual partition, the first part or function has to do with thinking, theory, or legitimacy. The second function has to so with doing, action, or power. The third function has to do with feeling, sustenance, or community; sustenance and community are related because the one is provided by the other.

This thesis was put forth by Georges Dumézil, in the middle of the twentieth century. He was a comparative linguist and cultural anthropologist teaching in France and Belgium; he died in 1986. It was based on a lot of evidence assembled over many years, almost wholly from ancient sources, for the most part mythological and sociological, all outside of biblical religion. The tripartite ideology survives in the modern world, though people don't often think of personal or social life as reflecting it prominently. Nevertheless, the tripartite ideology turns up in places where you would not expect it, and where it was not intended deliberately or consciously. Today, it is a habit of mind. Not the only habit of the modern mind in the West, but one that appears surprisingly often.

Look at Georges Dumézil's work on tripartite thinking, then apply it to what we have seen in the first two chapters, about affirmation of the world in Trinitarian form. We can unravel the process by which the Trinity grew out of the interaction of Jewish ideas and Hellenistic tripartite thinking. It has roots in both cultures, and reflects the system of tripartite thinking only imperfectly.

To my knowledge, nobody knows whether the connection between tripartite thinking and Indo-European language is accidental or intrinsic to the structures of the Indo-European languages. Some have argued that language shapes a culture's entire world. I think Dumézil did not, contenting himself with the prior task of substantiating the claim that tripartite ideology is in fact to be found peculiarly in the ancient Indo-European cultures in a significant way. This claim alone has been surprising enough to receive the prolonged critical attention of linguists and anthropologists. Doubtless further work is necessary in linguistics before anyone can hope to explain why the tripartite ideology is carried with Indo-European languages. The subject is hardly well defined even in terms of what is the phenomenon to be explained. It may be just an accident, it may be a disease of language, it may have many other as yet unimagined causes.

I need only a weaker claim than Dumézil makes, even though I think his claim may well be sustained. It is enough to notice that Indo-Europeans sometimes think in threes, with the functions we have outlined already. That the Trinity should be an example of this three-part organization should then come as no surprise.

A word of warning at the outset: Some doubtless will want to use the Indo-European tripartite ideology for racist purposes. Dumézil certainly did not, as his published comments on the Indo-Europeans make quite clear. He likened them to cannibals, and said that when you study cannibals, you should take good notes but stay out of the kitchen. I think he considered the tripartite ideology too confining, a sentiment that I certainly have shared from time to time. It is not so much a question of whether the tripartite organization of the world is a bug or a feature of Indo-European languages. (Some days I think it is a bug, some days I think it is a feature.) It is a question of whether it is a fact of life, something that is always present and available, whether one chooses to use it or not. In any case, it explains a fair amount of theological history, and that will be of no small help to us. In this and the next section, we look only at the bare structure of the tripartite ideology, and return to it in chapter 6, where we look at it again in the context of the problem of historical relativity.

## 3.2  Three-Part Worlds

The system works in pretty much the same way from India to Ireland. There are (or were; this is ancient history) three classes in society, and each class had gods to go with it.

## 3.2 Three-Part Worlds

At the top was the class in charge of knowledge. They decided what was real knowledge and what was not. More to the point, they decided what was legitimate and what was not, what was right and what was wrong. These were the priests and the lawyers. The priests were usually also the scientists. Things in Greece in the Hellenistic period were slightly modified. The first function division of labor was expanded and professional philosophers took over some of the work, but philosophy is a very first-function activity. Mathematics and science (meaning mostly astronomy) were associated with philosophy in those days.

There were two kinds of order, cosmic and juridical, meaning the order of the universe and the order of society. One god was in charge of each: in India, Varuna and Mitra, respectively. Juridical order means the maintenance of justice and the sanctity of contracts in civil society. Cosmic order means producing an explanation for the universe as a whole, and for man's place in it. Some of this structure has been lost in later Roman religion, but it was present at the beginning. The two gods of the first function were Jupiter and Dius Fidius; the latter has been forgotten. In the original Norse and German religion, the gods of the first function were Odin and Tyr.

The second function, in charge of action and administration, was also in charge of war and fighting. The king and the nobles are the leaders of this function. They are the aristocrats, they command the military, and they make the practical decisions in government. It is here that the Indo-European societies differed noticeably from their non-Indo-European neighbors, in Egypt and Mesopotamia, for example. For in those societies, there was no distinction between the first and second functions, and the king was also high-priest (and sometimes a god to boot). The Common Documents are somewhat confusing, because they inherited some Indo-European influences (from the Hittites) but did not speak an Indo-European language. In the Indo-European world, where war was distinguished from the first function, questions of legitimacy and order, there was generally one god in charge of war, with many helpers. In India, the war-god is Indra, and the helpers were the Maruts. In Rome, the war-god was Mars, in northern Europe, Thorr.

In the third function there were generally many gods. In India, Sarasvati and the Asvins. In Rome, Quirinus and Ops, from whose names we get the words "care" and "opulent." The third function in society was the work of farmers, artisans, craftsmen, healers, those who attend to nutrition and sustenance.

There was usually also a definite pecking order, and the classes are numbered in the order of status. The first function got what it wanted in its own department, and was sovereign in society. The second function had to defer to the first in matters of legitimacy and order, and as can be seen with a little reflection, legitimacy trumps practical decision making. The proverb that says "The pen is mightier than the sword" captures the relationship very neatly. This was not an easy settlement, and there has often been friction, with the second function challenging the first. It was that way in the middle ages in contests between the Papacy (first function) and the Holy Roman Emperor (second function). Or between Henry II and Thomas à Becket in England; Becket was murdered, but the Church won in the end anyway, and it had no force of its own, only moral authority. Or between Richard Nixon and Judge John Sirica; Sirica, the first-function figure, won.

Even the American Constitution is organized along tripartite lines, for Congress, the branch of government that raises the money, represents the third function (ways and means) and with it the mass of the people. The executive branch is the second function, in charge of getting things done and waging war. And the judiciary is the home of the first function. In the last half of the twentieth century, there have even been conflicts between the American judiciary and the other branches, much as has happened in earlier centuries and other Indo-European cultures.

India has always provided the clearest examples, and even today one can find recent Indian authors who champion the tripartite ideology unselfconsciously, without knowing much of its origins or the extent of its dispersion in the Indo-European world. The original organization tended to become confused as the centuries passed, and this happened in India as it did in the West. Vedic religion was the original religion in India. It was a world-affirming nature religion, and it lasted in more or less its original form until around 600 BCE. It displays the tripartite ideology fairly well. Later religion, the Hinduism of yoga and the Upanishads, is much less clear. It arose in social reforms around 600 BCE.

In Rome, things were much the same. Dius Fidius was obscured and Jupiter took over his work. Greek ideas were imported, and the twelve chief gods of later Roman religion did all the work of the three functions, but were not so cleanly compartmentalized. Greek religion seems to have lost its symmetry before the oldest surviving records, and while it shows traces of the tripartite system, it rarely if ever displayed it intact. Greek culture and literature outside of what we would call "religion" have more traces of the tripartite system than the myths of the gods do.

And the same sort of thing happens in the Trinity: creation is normally thought of as a second-function activity, but the Logos participates in it. Does the Logos actually create, or merely supervise? Theologians haven't worried about it much. Deciding what's right and what's wrong is normally a first-function activity, but it was done by God the Father, who decreed the laws for human beings to live by. There has been much exchange of tasks even in the Trinity. (For a few details, see Porter and Hobbs 1999).

## 3.3 Inversions

In some ways, religion among the ancient Indo-Europeans was much the same as it was in other ancient cultures, despite the different division of labor among the gods and again among professions in society. The gods each provide you with blessings in their own departments.

They bring the good things in life, and they show you how to get the good things in life. When life brings pain and disappointment, the gods are angry, and it is time to bribe them (if you can). It would not be a bad idea to bribe them anyway, ahead of time, just to stay on their good side. Those who fall foul of the gods are beyond help. Here, the truth *can't* do you any good when the truth hurts. Here, the ending in Camus' story is the only possible one; the mother and daughter were simply out of luck; there is nothing they could have done to recover from their sins.

Thus the gods of legitimacy help you control your legitimacy. The gods of order explain the order of the cosmos to you. But they are of little help when you are in the wrong, caught red-handed, or when the universe doesn't make much sense at all.

Simple power is the theme, control and how to get it. When your society is beaten by another, it's time to adopt the gods of the victors.

In fairness, this describes a late stage of ancient religion. In its original form, as a world-affirming nature religion, it was much like the shamanism that was the original religion world-wide. That religion was focused on nature, and its goals were to maintain the harmony of nature, to fit man into that harmony, and to restore that harmony when it was disrupted. To make this work, you have to understand nature in ways that for all their differences from modern science were also very similar: Nature is orderly and predictable, even in its disorderly upheavals, and that natural order is the key to making sense of human life and human action.

Two things happened as centuries rolled on and history first was remembered. One came with the coming of history itself, and the other with the advent of multi-national empires. History is not orderly, history is a sequence of accidents, of deliberate human actions that cannot be predicted as nature can. History is essentially disruptive to the order of nature, at least as it was experienced by ancient man. And so the original religions could not do much with history. How historical religion got started in the Bible is a story for another book. The other

## 3.3 Inversions

development, multi-national empires, merely created order at the cost of spreading misery and establishing the rule of the mighty over the weak. But they did one thing more—they provided an expanded horizon, an expanded world-view. They made it possible to see far enough so that history might make sense. If you have always lived in Podunk, and things have never changed in Podunk, history doesn't make much sense. If you know about the Big City, where things have changed, and if you know about *other* big cities, where things have not only changed, but have been different from *your* big city, then history becomes imaginable.

What happened when biblical religion was born? We have seen already—it began, slowly, to embrace the pains and disappointments of life, on the theory that they were not barren, but pregnant with blessing. (This was in *Waters*, chs. 6 and 7.) What happened when biblical religion moved from its Hebrew and Aramaic-speaking origins into the Greek-speaking world? Much the same thing: the pains of life now bear blessings, as we saw in Chapter Two.

In effect, in the Trinity the goals of the Indo-European system are *inverted*. To get control over your own legitimacy is to be able to stonewall exposure, to be protected or exempted from exposure. But instead of showing you how to defend yourself from exposure, the God of the Bible shows you how to embrace it. Now the truth really does do you some good even when it hurts.

Much the same thing happens in the other two functions. Limitation, even when it is terminal, bears blessing, life more abundantly (that's what the Resurrection was all about). The God does not show you how to get out of limitation, he shows you how to find blessing *in* limitation. And need, both material and spiritual, in the faces of strangers and foreigners, is now the doorway to new life in a different way, the way that comes from companionship, the not-alone-ness of a community that takes care of its members. This community was supposed to be open to all, and sometimes it has even lived up to its own standards.

This has deep roots in the Exodus and the social ethics of the early Monarchy, the time of David and Solomon and the years after them. For the Exodus and Deuteronomy, its social program, are quite repetitious about openness and generosity to strangers. Rabbinic Judaism has continued all these commitments in its own way, but without the Indo-European tripartite ideology, after the Temple in Jerusalem was destroyed in 70 CE.

An Indo-European racist ideology would require the tripartite system in its original form. It would be the religion of the gods who give you security, power, and wealth, the gods who show you how to stonewall exposure, how to dominate your neighbors and how to stiff them in their need. And white racism today does seem to be a way of securing legitimacy, getting control, and stiffing the needy neighbors. That's probably why Aryan racists who know what they are doing don't much like Christianity. (The ones who are seriously confused think the God of the New Testament is on their side, and will bring them exemption from exposure, limitation, and need. They have to think Jesus was not Jewish, but instead was an Aryan.)

In the original form, the gods of the first function help the righteous and arrange the punishment of the sinners, but in the inverted Trinitarian form, the God in the first function helps the sinners, because the righteous don't need any help. In the original form of the second function, the gods help the strong, and they may help you become strong, if they like you. In the inverted form, the God helps the weak. In the original form, the gods provide for the wealthy; in the inverted form, the God is on the side of the poor.

In its transformed and inverted biblical form, things are different with the tripartite conceptual scheme. Nobody is supposed to be in control of the truth, and no ethnic group is supposed to lord it over everybody else. And society is now supposed to be open to outsiders, even (especially!) to non-Indo-Europeans. Eventually, that means getting outside of the tripartite ideology and learning to think the biblical inversion of values in the idiom of other cultures.

# Chapter 4

# But Why?

## 4.1 Because it's There

When someone asked George Leigh Mallory why he wanted to climb Mt. Everest, he answered, "Because it's there." It seemed obvious to Mallory—though not to many others. And since Mallory never succeeded, what was the point? But it was a very effective way to put an end to further questioning.

When people ask you why you are doing whatever it is you are doing, what do you answer? When they think it is of dubious worth, what do you answer? When they think you are crazy to do it, what do you answer? When it seems obvious to you, and equally obvious that it will never be obvious to them, what do you answer? When you have run out of answers, what do you answer?

When people ask, "Why embrace exposure, limitation, and need," what do you answer? "Because they are there?" What would *that* answer mean?

Mallory's answer probably doesn't fit in too many situations other than his own. The street language that comes naturally is something a little different, more like, "Because that's where it's *at*, man!"

Driven to frustration with questioning, unable to supply the sort of justification that your tormenter wants, you still have to say something. When you say something like "Because that's where it's *at*," you have made what is both an answer and a commitment. In a way, it is a take-it-or-leave-it answer. The other person may come over and see what it's really like to do what you're doing, or he may not. In any case, you have made a challenge and an invitation as well as just an answer to the question. Your example challenges, your words invite.

There is a technical term for this sort of talk: it is a *confessional* statement, because in it, one confesses a commitment. Evidently it is a fairly big commitment, because you are talking about doing something that is worthwhile for its own sake, and possibly something that is life-shaping. Your life has some sort of basic orientation, basic sense of direction, basic sense of what's worthwhile and what's not. The activity that elicited your friend's question "Why?" is emblematic of your life's basic direction.

But back to exposure, limitation, and need, and the dubious wisdom of embracing them in hopes of finding something good in them. It would be best to answer delicately.

For if you just say yes, you expect to find blessings in them, you are shooting your mouth off—in a big way. You have made promises you are in no position to keep, because you have no idea what pains life may bring. You don't know what it will take to embrace them, you don't know whether you have what it takes. And as we saw from Albert Camus' story about the innkeeping family out in the boonies, you can easily be destroyed, even by exposure; never mind limitation or need.

So there is a certain seriousness about this kind of "that's where it's at, man." Your life is on the line. But there ought to be some seriousness in this sort of question, because in the end, you have only one life to live, and you live it *for* something, namely, for the activities you engage in. Are they worth it? Do they bring lasting satisfaction? Was it time well spent? Now merely being "serious" won't necessarily make you serious—for maybe you should have relaxed more, had more

## 4.1 Because it's There

fun, sung in Gilbert and Sullivan, or become a Monty Python fan. So effort alone won't cut it, however much effort may help.

And how would you *tell* what's worthwhile and what's not? Especially when we're talking about embracing exposure, limitation, and need? Not a very promising prospect, if I may say so.

In the end, you are compared to other people. People can see what you did, and what other people did. You will be compared with people who *have* embraced exposure, limitation, and need, at great cost to themselves. If you rejected the pains of life as barren where others found life more abundantly in them, what then?

There is no proof that all of life is good, pains included, and I don't think there can be. But the comparisons do show something; they tell what's going on in people's lives. Such a comparison is itself a form of exposure, and it can itself be embraced or rejected.

Now this is noticeably circular reasoning: if you think it is a good idea to embrace exposure, you will see yourself and your life one way; if you don't, your life will appear quite differently. If you *do* embrace exposure, and live in a way that is open to exposure, you will live differently from those who close off the truth. If you do embrace the truth, even when it hurts, you will think it was worthwhile. If you don't, and stonewall it, you will also think that move gave you real freedom. But a very different kind of "real" freedom. Either way, you will think you made the right choice.

You are asked in the end, by the pains of life themselves, whether life as it really is is really worth it. And you have to answer for yourself. No fair claiming to have a proof, and just quoting the proof. Contrary to rumors that have been around for a few hundred years, The Bible doesn't have any proofs, though that is not a story for this book. The great assembly at Shechem in Joshua 24 is the paradigm of the choice of faith. Joshua says to the assembled Israelites, "Which gods will you serve? ... as for me and mine, ... "

In the end, when people ask you (or you ask yourself) why it is right to take all of life as good, pains included, you answer, "Because that's the way things are."

## 4.2 That's The Way Things Are

So how are things, really? Is this really The Way Things Are? Things might have been otherwise. There might have been no world at all. The world might not be a good place, life might not really be good after all. The pains might make life defective, and then you should strike the best bargain you can, avoid the pains, get as much of the gold (or sex, or whatever) as you can, share it with a few chosen friends, and devil take the hindmost.

Or if life is *really* defective, you should try to get out of it as fast as you can. That's hard, since suicide isn't fun. But there are ways to get out of it while still being in it, if you get my drift. You can live on the basis of the worthlessness of life, and for the worth of something else, something better. Escapism can take many forms.

For another alternative, I was once reproached by a dear friend for doing something "unnatural" when I had put ketchup on egg rolls. I smirked and said, "I'm a child of nature, and everything I do is natural." In other words, this exposure thing is madness; just be a part of nature. Nature will take care of you. Leg-pulling though I was, that answer is pretty close to the mark for a nature-oriented life.

So how are things, really? Given that life might have been otherwise (assuming that you *do* think it is all good, simply because it is there), what do you make of the goodness of life? Sometimes it looks very fragile, very precarious. How do you respond to it? How do you make sense of it?

Why do exposure, limitation, and need bring grace, creativity, and fellowship? "Because that's just the way things are" is not a bad answer, as answers go. I suppose a technical term for the same thing would be just "ultimate reality," though you can't do quite so much with it. Still, if you bend your ear, both phrases will work in ways that might surprise you.

Ultimate reality may be quite different from how you think it is. There is a gamble in the commitment of living for one way of thinking about life instead of another, and that gamble cannot be avoided. If you think you have proofs that one way to live is the right way, instead of another, those proofs have a way of wilting under criticism. Other people will just say, "that's the way *you* think things are." And they are right. But the phrase "The Way Things Are," capitalized to make it clear that you have a big stake in it, is a phrase that avoids a host of problems and confusions.

In the first place, as we have seen, it makes it clear that life-orientation is a confessional commitment, not something that could be proven or disproven. It is also clear that you can get a pretty good idea of what somebody lives for. And people can be compared, so you can't escape making some judgements. It is not as if there is no possibility of criticism, it is not as if lacking proof, we are left with only taste, caprice, and whimsy as guides to life. Those who will look can see; those who will listen can hear.

## 4.3 Hidden In Plain Sight

Since the high Middle Ages, Christianity has had more than ordinary trouble explaining itself. Behind the problem of proof was the problem of how God could be both in the world and out of this world. Explaining to outsiders and skeptics has been hard enough; explaining to insiders has not been very successful either.

The phrase "The Way Things Are," taken as a name for God, avoids most of these problems.

"The Way Things Are" is not a something that might or might not exist. The Way Things Are is not a description of the world—this is not pantheism. It was originally the answer to a question, the end (or start) of questioning: why is it the right thing to do, the right way to live, embracing exposure, limitation, and need? Why do they bring blessing? Because that's the way things are. Capitals get added later, when people begin to suspect that there is more here than meets the eye.

The Way Things Are is not an expression that engages reality by *referring* to a thing or to a feature of reality that could be inspected or verified objectively. It does indeed engage reality—but in a way that only street language can. It is an answer to a question, and that question is about the worth of human life and the worth of a certain approach to human life. It is an answer that we test in living, not in theory or science of any kind. And it is fragile: this language can always be broken precisely by treating it as if it were technical language, referring to something that could be objectivated.

As a first consequence, we don't have to worry about the "existence of God," proofs for it, or disproofs of it. A small industry in the philosophy of religion is obsolete. And we don't have the problems that come after such proofs, namely making sense of God as "a" being, one among other beings, supreme or otherwise. How would one being have omnipotent control over every other being? That's no longer a sensible question, and it needs no more worry.

How can "The Way Things Are" be omnipotent (or for that matter, less than omnipotent)? As omnipotence was usually understood, that meant a willful mind that could make things be or happen one way instead of another. That conception no longer makes sense, and with it, unnecessary parts of the so-called "problem of evil" will go away, as we shall see. For now, how could we have come to call The Way Things Are "omnipotent"? Only by analogy—and only by analogies that we have created ourselves. Clearly (leaving aside doubts as to just *how* things are), The Way Things Are is not something that we can bargain with or influence or control. It was just this human lack of bargaining power that was expressed in the language of "omnipotence," though that language is for the most part later than the Bible. There are roots of it in Deutero-Isaiah, you can find it in the enthronement Psalms (95-100), and doubtless other places also. In the Bible, it was never the developed philosophical concept that it became in later

## 4.3 Hidden In Plain Sight

Greek-speaking theology.

Look again at what "omnipotence" means: the omnipotent one is the one who is not subject to limitation, who can "do anything," do anything he wants. The Way Things Are is more like just the limitations themselves than it is like anyone subject—or not subject—to limitation. It doesn't even make sense to ask whether limitation is subject to limitation. If we personify The Way Things Are by analogy in order to speak to it, in order to commit ourselves, we should remember the limits of the analogy. When we forget, trouble happens real fast. As the one who is not subject to limitation, the traditional "God" became a model for human life and human action: seek to avoid limitation, because that's what "God" does. People then prayed to that "God," asking it to get them out of limitation. Exposure was not seen, and need was stiffed, as usual.

How can The Way Things Are be omniscient? How can it know everything? (How can it even know *anything*?) To put things at their most perplexing, how can it *fore*-know everything? How can it know what human beings *would* have done under circumstances other than those that actually happen? None of these questions make sense. The Way Things Are is spoken of as knowing anything at all only by analogy. This language expresses human ignorance and human trust more than it expresses any theory of divine knowledge. In fact, it avoids any theory of divine knowledge.

How can The Way Things Are be in time? Or eternal? The Way Things Are is not something that lives in time; it is much more nearly like Augustine's conception of God outside of time, God as creator of time. But when we normally try think of God outside of time, as we read about God in the *Confessions*, we naturally think of God as being in his "own" time, separate from ours. This was the analogy that Dorothy Sayers used when she likened our time to the time *within* a fictional story, with the author outside of that time and the story. And authors do come into the story sometimes, and not only incognito; Kurt Vonnegut once did. But if we think of God as The Way Things

Are, none of these problems arise.

How could The Way Things Are act in the world? How could there be divine acts at all, if we are to think of God as The Way Things Are? Is it a cause in nature? Is it an actor in history? Yes and No; not exactly, in both cases. It depends on how you understand the language of action. Is The Way Things Are present and visible in nature and history? Most assuredly—for who could not be amazed and awed at the way nature works, or at how things unfold in history? So The Way Things Are can certainly elicit the kind of awe, sense of human smallness, and simultaneous yearning and fear that are the marks of the holy.

What about history? How can we have mighty acts of God in history, if we think of God as just The Way Things Are? It's not as hard as you might think. If it really is right to embrace all of life as good, this "rightness" should show itself in events, in how history plays out. (This is called "particular acts of God.") Do those who embrace exposure, limitation, and need really find life more abundantly? Were they right to do so? If so, you have seen The Way Things Are as it shows itself in events. That's what people call the mighty acts of God in history.

What happens when people's lives are changed, transformed, by surprises in history? When poetic justice finally happens, when windfalls come, with life more abundantly? How would you fit such an event and the phrase "The Way Things Are" into the same sentence? Usually, you would just say "That's the way things are." But what if you were to say, "The Way Things Are has set things right, done justice, told it like it is, filled the hungry with good things and sent the rich empty away?" Odd, but striking. What about when poetic justice does *not* happen? When it is delayed, when people languish or die for lack of justice, as happens all the time? We cry out for justice, hoping that TWTA will show itself. What that means is that we are confident that it really is right to embrace the limitations of life as blessing-bearing, even when we are destroyed by them. This will not

## 4.3 Hidden In Plain Sight

be an easy faith.

I have no doubt that the language of "the way things are" can be broken, twisted to purposes other than these. (Trivially, it will be broken when it is taken not as the answer to a forgotten question but as a description of the world. That way leads to Neoplatonism or pantheism or the like.) But it cannot be broken in the same old ways, not in the usual way that talk about acts of God gets into trouble. Those who are reckless or foolhardy ask *how* God acts, and then try to guess the physics of divine actions. Instead, we can say, That's just the way things are, and now you can see what counts and what doesn't, who's real and who's phony. You can see life more abundantly for those who embrace it as a whole.

How could we speak of God as "outside" the world, or (pardon the technical term) "transcendent" to the world, and simultaneously "immanent," present within the world? The Way Things Are is not a something within the world. It is also not a something "outside" the world, and here is the way to get out of most of the puzzles of transcendence. For something, a "thing," that is "outside" the world can easily be sucked into the world just by moving the fence that separates the world from whatever is outside it. And lo! That something is now within the world, no longer transcendent. (Put in another way, it is not at all obvious what it would even mean for a thing or being to be "outside" the world.) But thinking of transcendence as something "outside" the world was not really a very good way to think of transcendence in the first place. Yet The Way Things Are is clearly transcendent to the world, just because it is not a thing within the world, and being "outside" the world doesn't make sense.

It is not something that you could get a firm conceptual grip on. You can name it only in the most loose and tentative way. It won't come when you call it, though we have to call it. It may very well come when you don't call it. It's always there, but it is invisible, not at your disposal. It is not something that you could speak for, though sometimes we must. It is not a tame concept, not domesticated.

The notion of The Way Things Are as a way to speak about God avoids other problems in thinking about divine acts. For people traditionally tend to think that if God is to come into the world and act, he has to cut a hole in the world in order to fit in (or create a world with pre-cut and uncloseable holes already in it). The world has to make way, make space for God to act. Divine causes have to *substitute* for physical causes, or else God cannot act, because to do anything, he has to push on something to get it to move, just like I do when I step on the gas in my car.

This is to take language of divine acts literally, and it is also to use a very naturalistic model of human actions as the model for the literal interpretation. If, instead, we think of The Way Things Are as acting, we can do so only in analogies. They are highly ironic analogies—for TWTA is not a thing that could literally act, and if we speak of it as acting (as we must), we know that our analogies are not literally true. And these are analogies that can't easily be bent into the same old literal ruts where divine action requires God to cut a hole in the world in order to push on something in order to make it alter course. The language of TWTA really *is* about transcendence and immanence, both at the same time: The natural and worldly processes of the world are not disturbed, and yet TWTA acts in the world nonetheless.

One might ask where such a God is, where is "The Way Things Are"? To that question there is no answer. It doesn't make sense.

What is it about life that we mean when we say "that's The Way Things Are"? Obviously, in my own highly opinionated opinion, it is the affirmation of human life in full view of its pains, without sentiment, without self-deception, without saccharin, without denial. It was like the closing song in Monty Python's *The Life of Brian*: "Always look on the bright side of life," a song that also offended many and delighted many more, and for very much the same reasons. I hear my own theology in it. But I am as clueless as the next joe, and so I am shooting my mouth off—as anyone must be, who proposes to embrace life as good in full view of its pains. The proper response was

## 4.3 Hidden In Plain Sight

just to laugh. Alas, in present circumstances, trying to make sense of theology, that's not quite enough. (Laughter is forbidden in theology.)

Faced with transcendence, what then becomes of the question, "Where *is* God?" We get turned back, to look at ourselves. For the question could be better put as "Where is God *when I need him?*" That puts the human involvement front and center. It is not a question just about God in some theoretical and detached mode. The answer is the answer that came from the burning bush: "I will be who I will be," in the words of one recent translation (William Propp, Anchor Bible Exodus). Not really an answer to Moses' question, and not entirely reassuring. We shall see another translation of this text momentarily.

# Chapter 5

# Who Turned The Lights Out?

## 5.1 Panic

If a wording like "The way things are" works this way and avoids so many problems, why don't we talk this way? Why do we accept all the problems with the traditional explanations, without looking for something better? What is it about the traditional explanations that made them so attractive in spite of their problems?

I think people wanted to have a god at their disposal, conceptual disposal at least, a god visible to the mind's eye. Such a god is more comforting than trying to talk to The Way Things Are. Such a god is more likely to give you what you want than is The Way Things Are. The Way Things Are is a little *too* omnipotent, a little too powerful. The Way Things Are is impossible to bargain with. The Way Things Are is also too shrouded in mystery. For starters, you can't really tell *how* things are. What limitations hold is rarely obvious. Often, you find real limitations only by struggling with them. But The Way Things Are is mysterious at a deeper level also. For who could wrap his mind around the whole universe? Who could wrap her mind around even the whole reality of the local human situation, whatever it is?

So there are grounds for discomfort with such a name for God. (Or perhaps better, "God" is just a name for ultimate reality, for The Way Things Are.) Even so, there are precedents for talking this way. In the job interview with Moses in Exodus 3, God doesn't appear; there is only a burning bush and a voice. Nothing visible. And the difference between seeing and hearing is important. For when we see, we can turn what we see into an object, something that is under conceptual control. When we hear but do not see, we are called, or better, summoned, and we have to answer—but to what?

That story, the burning bush, has more in it than one might think in its choice of an image for God that is not really visible, but instead can only be heard. It comes out in Moses' final question, "Who *are* you?" God gives an answer, if the Hebrew can be paraphrased, that is more than a little paradoxical: "I shall be with you as who I am shall I be with you." Moses' basic anxiety is now out in the open: will he (and we) be alone, abandoned, or will he (and we) have some comfort? The voice from the bush is not entirely reassuring. John Courtney Murray is scathing in describing what we want: The God of the Exodus "is not the functional God of contemporary immanentist theory and its theologically decadent taste—a God whose function is to respond to man's religious needs and satisfy his spiritual aspirations." (Murray, p. 12.)

Murray's version of Exodus 3.14, "I shall be with you as who I am shall I be with you," is not in the text of any translation that I've ever seen. Some have "I will be who I will be," and that gets us out of a philosopher's fascination with ontology and the mystery of Being, but it's still not quite what the commentator heard in Exodus 3.14. Murray gave us a meditation on what the obscure Hebrew text means in human terms. (The translators have pronounced themselves more than a little perplexed by what to do with *eyeh asher eyeh*, the text that he took liberties with.) God doesn't tell Moses his name. He just says he will be with Moses—and Israel—and they shouldn't worry about it. But of course worry about it is exactly what they do. And so do we. For we always ask, "Where is God when we need him?"

Usually at this point, theologians and philosophers say that we can't really know anything about God, and then they go on to say a great deal about God. (One might fairly feel somewhat in the dark here.) That we can say nothing positive about God and still talk about God is called the via negativa. That we can nevertheless say a great deal positive about God is called the method of analogy. That tradition is old, and technical. It is widely respected, and for good reason. Despite its merits, I would like to come to it slowly. When people move too quickly to analogy, it is easy to miss how analogies work, and to miss the hazards, the audacity, and the genius of analogy.

Instead of looking next at how God "is with" us, it would make better sense to look at how we are alone. For that is the appearance, and there is a great deal of truth in that appearance. What does "alone" mean? Different things to different people, no doubt. In the commonest meaning of being not-alone, namely, that there is "a" "being" present with us, though invisible, we are indeed alone. For my money, there is no such being. I want no part of a theology whose God is an undetectable entity that interferes with the natural course of events to the advantage of those who think it exists and the disadvantage of those who do not. (Much technical philosophy and theology are about this undetectable entity, but surprisingly often, popular theology, though untheoretical, does better.) Before progress is possible, it is necessary to deepen the sense of aloneness (hopefully not panic) that comes when you give up the god whom Murray denounced—the cosmic concierge, chief of Room Service, who answers our every wish and spiritual aspiration.

## 5.2  Atheists Who Believe in God

It probably comes as a surprise that Christians and Jews were regarded as atheists by their neighbors in the ancient world. Now the word "atheist" is quite old, unlike "religious." There was no word for religion or religious until the Romans made one up as a way to both fool and pacify their subjects. In other words, you can have whatever "religion" you like—so long as your basic life orientation puts the Emperor ahead of everything else. (Render unto Caesar what is Caesar's, and you can have what's left.) But basic life orientation is a round-about term for religion, as we can see now. There were words in ancient languages for piety, but piety is not quite the same thing as the modern concept of religion. And there were not words for "theist" or "theists," not in quite the way that recent philosophy of religion thinks of Christians and Jews.

The word *atheos*, the Greek word for atheist, had more than one meaning. You can of course dismiss the meanings you don't like, and so turn the ancient pagan rejection of Christians and Jews into a charge of being just "not-pagan." Then the ancients are just like us, there is nothing new under the sun, and nothing disturbs our own preconceptions of what it means to be religious (and especially what it means to be biblically religious).

I would like to take at face value one of the odder meanings of the word. It appears in a few texts, so we know the word had this usage in more than just one place. Here, the Hellenistic pagans believed in god(s), where Jews and Christians did not. The accusation is not just that biblical religion disagreed with its neighbors about *which* gods to worship, but that it had *no* god(s) *at all*.

In the Hellenistic world, worshipers of different gods each allowed the others' gods a certain kind of worth, as a professional courtesy. Part of the complaint against Christians was merely that they refused to participate in this reciprocity. In other words, the game was, "you scratch my back, and I'll scratch yours," and Christians and Jews wouldn't play. Christians were obnoxious about it; I think Jews were more diplomatic.

But I think there is another meaning in the charge of atheism, a more literal meaning that sees something profound about biblical religion and takes fright and rejects it. Remember that the Temple in Jerusalem had no statue of the God in it. One has to see temples that

## 5.2 Atheists Who Believe in God 53

*do* have statues of the gods in them to appreciate just how beautiful such sacred architecture is. And so the Temple in Jerusalem must have stood out in the surrounding culture. Matters are somewhat ambiguous, because the Jews had no difficulty *praying* to this invisible God. But there was something definitely peculiar about it (or him), and the empty Temple says as much. As far as the pagan mind could understand, if there was no image, there was nothing there. It might as well have been an empty room in the center of the Temple. A few loaves of bread, a box of heirlooms, and some lampstands don't make up for the missing image.

In effect, Israelite religion was a high-church atheism. At least it was when it lived up to its own standards, and Ezekiel certainly tells us that often it did not. Such a temple was meant to make you feel uneasy. Such a temple was a way of keeping alive the feeling from the interview at the burning bush, when God answers Moses' request for a name with just "I shall be with you as who I am shall I be with you."

Why the panic? Why the anxiety? What's wrong with worshiping a god that's not there? Art has a way of showing what's going on when it's not entirely obvious.

Look again at the reciprocity of the Hellenistic religions. Each of those religions was, if you will, a strategy for living, a strategy for finding happiness, a strategy for getting what you want. The non-reciprocity of Judaism and Christianity was a way of saying to all those religions, such strategies do not work. At all. The anxiety was quite appropriate—in face of a religion where the God is useless when you want to escape the pains of life.

It is too upsetting to think that something could bring good when all your strategies for finding good fail. What if good came when things look really black, in and through the failure of all attempts to find happiness? Not because a strategy surprised you and succeeded, but after all our strategies failed? What if the causes for which we live all die? And good still comes, in and through that failure of all our efforts?

It took a long time for a theologian to be that simple, that in-your-face about it. It's in the Bible, of course: for the prophets repeatedly told little Israel and littler Judah that disaster was coming, usually "from the north," i.e, from Assyria or Babylon, who would attack coming south from Syria rather than directly across the desert through what is today Jordan. And people heard the prophets, and believed them; disaster *was* coming. But what the people could not hear, what made no sense, was the idea that the God who had brought them out of Egypt in the Exodus could bring them anything good in such a disaster. Deutero-Isaiah, the Isaiah of the Exile, said the same thing again about the return from Babylon. Then people believed, some, though they grumbled, just as their forefathers had grumbled on the way out of Egypt. And both the rabbis and the Jesus movement said it again after the disasters of the first century, especially the destruction of the Temple by the Romans in 70 CE.

As later theologians thought about it, the idea was certainly there. H. Richard Niebuhr, half Lutheran, half Calvinist, teaching at Yale from the 1930s to the early 1960s, said it in so many words. "The causes for which we live all die." Perhaps the Calvinists, most impressed with the "power" of God, were the ones who influenced Niebuhr. Perhaps it was experiences in his own life, and observations of the world around him. Allow me a trip through his meditation on disaster and hope; it is in a short essay on the concept of God, "Faith in Gods and in God," in an appendix to *Radical Monotheism and Western Culture*, p. 122.

For what one age thinks will bring happiness passes in another age. What you think will work today fails tomorrow. Empires and cities all decay, sooner or later. More to the point, and sooner, too, we all die, merely as individuals. We all try to evade this knowledge, but we know it's true nonetheless. Niebuhr liked to quote Bertrand Russell in a particularly black mood: "on us and all our race the slow, sure doom falls pitiless and dark." More people than just Niebuhr have quoted

## 5.2 Atheists Who Believe in God

Russell in this passage; it was an eye-stopper. Russell was no prophet, he promised no salvation in or through or after the doom. Just doom. And so Russell is a good spokesman for the reception this doom gets naturally, instinctively, in each and every one of us—at first. When you see the coming doom, you have more choices than might be apparent at the start.

Think about it. Denial is the natural first response. Do the causes we live for *really* all die? If you think you have an exception, if you think you know a way to live so that in the end you can avoid exposure, limitation, and need, you would not still be reading this book. But denial is always possible.

Bargaining follows when denial won't work any more. It is natural to think you can work out a deal. (This book is pointless if you actually can.)

Why should the causes for which we live all die? Look at what Niebuhr says: "We may call it the nature of things, we may call it fate, we may call it reality." Remarkably close to the "That's The Way Things Are" that we stumbled on some pages ago! There may be no name for it. You can just call it "void," or "Void," with a capital-V, if you feel reverent before it. Really, it has no name; God's answer to Moses at the burning bush is right on the money: You have no name for me, but I will be with you.

Whatever this reality is, there is no fighting it in the end, for it overwhelms us in the end. Niebuhr gives voice to our inevitable shock at the idea of embracing the defeat of all our causes—the idea that that defeat could bear blessing. Nevertheless, this is not the cause for despair that it might appear to be, nor does it mean that all is fated, nothing can be changed. If there is no fighting it in the end, there is much to be gained by wrestling with it in the meantime—in trust and in hope, not despair and defiance. Isra-el is the one who struggles with God (Genesis 32). As the story goes, Jacob, renamed Israel, limps away with a badly strained hip, but also with a blessing. How does it work? This phenomenon, enduring reality though it be, is more like an uncanny series of coincidences than it is like the consistent action of a single actor. But it is consistent, if only because it is patient. If you look for a single reason for the defeat of all our causes and for the accompanying blessings, you will find nothing. There is only that uncanny pattern of coincidences. When we see it, we say, with Job, "Though it slay us, yet will we trust it."

Kind of hits the nail on the head, doesn't it? Sort of pours warm flat beer on any lingering delusions, doesn't it? But it's what radical monotheism is all about, from the beginning before the Exodus to the present, and to wherever it will go from here.

That's what exposure, limitation, and need are all about. They are what happens to the causes we used to live for. They are what happens when a project fails. Exposure, limitation, and need are unwelcome good news.

Niebuhr didn't get much hoopla. The French existentialists did; they were notorious, *enfants terribles*. They declared that we are alone in the universe, the meaning of life is not to be found in nature, all we can do is choose. The human situation is radical choice in barren and absurd loneliness. They dropped from on high into the twentieth century to spread doubt, despondency and existential anomie among unsuspecting sensible folks everywhere. Hot chatter about the absurd nature of life and man's lonely isolation in the universe.

If they had taken the last chapter of Joshua instead of Psalm 14.1 as their guide to philosophy of religion, they would have known that (a) radical choice was seen long, long ago, and (b) the "existence" of God is not the interesting question. The great French existentialists were not very original. It's in the Bible, if anybody had the sense to look in the right place. So what's going on when we think we are alone, abandoned? The anxiety expressed in the name of God, "I shall be with you as who I am shall I be with you"? When that name names our feeling that he is *not* with us? Which god is it that has abandoned us? Not the God of the Bible but the god of Christian Platonism, the god who is "a" "being," an undetectable entity that interferes with the natural course of events to the advantage of those who think it exists and the disadvantage of those who do not.

Still, to give credit where it is due, few read Joshua at all, and of those who do, few hear what the covenant renewal in chapter 24 really means about God and philosophy. The French existentialists rediscovered it, and they don't fare any better than Joshua. Few listen to them and fewer hear.

So if God is here with us, then how is he here with us? That's the next question. How are we to recognize the immanent presence of—of what? Let's just call it transcendence, in order not to prejudice questions about *what* God is.

## 5.3 The Far Side

There is a phrase from common language, "The Other Side," and people use it when they mean they are talking to departed spirits. So-and-so has gone over to the Other Side. And there was a one-panel cartoon late in the twentieth century called "The Far Side," drawn by Gary Larson. We saw it, briefly, in *Waters*, in "Tickets to Bali H'ai." It's worth returning to. Both of the phrases "The Far Side" and "The Other Side" mean, in their own way, transcendence, for transcendence just means crossing over, whether to the other side or to the far side. But the common phrase and the cartoon have somewhat different ideas about human life. You don't *see* any other side in The Far Side. All you *see* is this world. A twisted world, some of Larson's friends and readers thought, but it is still just *this* world. Or so it seems.

By contrast, the Other Side is like a telephone call: with help from a psychic or a medium, you can talk to people on the Other Side. The Other Side is pop-platonism, the view that says people are made of a discardable body and a detachable soul. When somebody dies, his or her soul goes someplace. You can still talk to it, if you have the right kind of professional help. I can't rule out such a dualist view of ultimate reality, but it is not a view that holds much attraction for me, and my purpose here is to explore another way.

Let me meditate on The Far Side, for it shows us the immanent presence of a certain kind of transcendence. It lacks a great deal: there is no sense of the brokenness of human life, and there is no sense of history. The brokenness of life can be seen in another one-panel cartoon, "Close to Home," in which people do unconscionable things to each other. You have to laugh, but it is a slightly uncomfortable laugh. In The Far Side, you identify with every actor, both victims and perpetrators. It is a fair window into world-affirming nature religion, and it is also a fair window into the beginnings of human creaturehood. Out of that grows world-affirming historical religion, when people see that they have to face the discomforts of "Close to Home."

That should tell us something: transcendence is visible in nature, if you know where to look, even though latter-day nature religions sometimes don't like to admit it. There is pain enough in The Far Side, and if you want to affirm its world, whether you know it or not, when you laugh, you are bumping into the immanent presence of transcendence. There is no other way to affirm life when you are about to be destroyed. And there is destruction enough in nature, without the brokenness that human life in history is uniquely capable of.

Pardon all the technical language. Transcendence is what crosses over, to something else. Immanence is like its shadow in this world, or its this-worldly presence. If you do it right, there is no transcendence without immanence, so you are not in any danger of having a transcendent that you can't get to. (Actually, you don't have to get to it, you can't get to it, but it comes to you. That is enough.)

I once ran into a definition of creaturehood that runs something like this: to be a creature is to be finite, not in control. Often enough, a creature reacts by trying to get in control, and that way lies trouble. The problems of not being in control are then aggravated. We love The Far Side because implicitly, all the creatures in it, human, animal, and alien alike, are somehow comfortable in their creaturehood, even as they try to get out of the limitations of creaturehood and regain

## 5.3 The Far Side

control over their lives. That's what we identify with. (We revisit to the brokenness of human life, briefly, when we come to unanswerable questions.)

They are somehow blessed in spite of the fact that they are about to be destroyed, or their plans overturned, or their pretenses unmasked. That blessedness doesn't come from any cause or actor within the world of The Far Side. That is just the way the world of The Far Side is. Whatever makes it be that way, if you don't take the language too literally, is something that transcends the actors and events of the comic strip. If you *do* take the language literally, then of course you are dealing with a deity that is undetectable but interferes with the natural course of events to inject blessing. But for the comic strip, the point is that the blessing does *not* come by interference, it's always already there, part of the world. And it is not an exception to what is natural, it *is* the natural.

What are your options? You could ignore or deny this kind of transcendence. That way leads back to a different kind of world-affirming nature religion. But as The Far Side attests, transcendence will come, whether it is called or not. Today we see enough of the sort of scientism that pretends to deny any and all transcendence. It then sneaks out when people are not looking, like a kid smoking behind the barn, and looks up at the night sky in raptures of awe and delight. Or it enjoys the funny-papers, unaware that it is cheating on its commitment to make sense of all human life in terms of only the natural sciences. You can subvert transcendence by, as I say, taking its language to mean interference from outside. You can just laugh—probably the best course, at least for the comic strip. But in laughing, you have acknowledged that you, too, are what theologians call a "creature," one whose plans are about to be upset. But the import of the comic strip, for those who can bear to reflect on it in so theoretical a fashion, is that our lives fit into a larger context that is humorous. The world we live in is the world of a joke, if the comic strips are telling the truth about life.

Subverting transcendence by taking its language literally and talking about interference from outside is the way of dualism. Dualisms are usually Platonist, meaning that there is another world in parallel to ours, and it is populated by demons, angels, pure concepts called Ideal Forms, the deity, and so on. But existence in that dual world is basically like existence in this world. Indeed, when you die, your soul goes to the dual world. What happens in this worldview? Transcendence gets domesticated, in the word of William Placher. It can no longer really challenge. It has been tamed. And you are on the way to getting out of limitation, rather than looking for the blessings in limitation. That's what outside interference was supposed to do. (Exposure and need get upstaged and not seen.)

It gets worse. If you are trying to get out of limitation, then the world you are living in here and now is not such a good world after all. And so pretty soon, you are not just trying to get out of limitation, you are trying to get out of this world. Or you are looking forward to getting out of it when you die. And Platonism provides the idea that people are composed of a discardable body and a detachable soul, so getting out should be pretty easy. This is the way to Gnosticism. In the ancient world, the Gnostics saw this world as defective, a hate-joke perpetrated by an incompetent semi-deity whom they were often pleased to identify with the God of the Common Documents. Some revivals of that Gnosticism can even be found on the Internet today.

Or, if you still want to affirm human life in this world, and you also want to take the language of transcendence literally, meaning you want an outside God who interferes on your behalf, then you are back in the land of theological naturalism. For here, the deity makes things happen by pushing on them, just like you make the car go by pushing on the gas pedal. Acts of God presumably mean the God pushes on things in the world, and they move to places they would not if left to natural causes alone. That is to say that you can in principle make sense of acts of God in naturalistic language, because you could see the difference between the natural motions of bodies and their motions

## 5.3 The Far Side

under the influence of divine action. This way also lies evasion of limitation. We wanted to get out of that theology in the beginning of *By the Waters of Naturalism*.

What else can you do? Are you left speechless before transcendence? No, not really.

For only one example of transcendence that we can speak about, why is the cosmos orderly? Why is the cosmos intelligible? There is not really any answer to these questions. (Let these stand as examples of *unanswerable* questions that are undeniable in contemporary culture; we shall see more in a few pages.) We can say a great deal about particular places that display the order of nature, but that is not just what the question asks about. We can even talk some about order in general in the natural world, and about the human enterprise in which we find order in the natural world. All without ever really answering the question. Why the cosmos is orderly is not a question that science can answer, though scientists can answer it after a fashion. That is because the order that the question has in mind does not appear as a term in any theory. How could it? It would have to encompass everything from physics to neurophysiology, and it's not likely that any single concept of order could do that. In any case, the scientists whose results produce so much awe are incidentally human, and it is as human beings that they stand in awe of their results, an awe that defies expression in any scientific theory. As human beings, they do know more than just science, and they know something from experience about human life. To ask why the cosmos is orderly is not a question *in* science but rather a question *about* science. It is a different kind of question about the world than the questions that are asked *in* science. Even then, it is not clear that there can be any answer to the question why the natural world is orderly. Like the commitment to embrace the pains of life as blessing-bearing, the order of the cosmos just is; it is the way things are. Questioning stops here.

## 5.4 Five Easy Pieces

Thomas Aquinas is famous, especially in freshman philosophy courses, for the "five ways of proving the existence of God." Actually, the Latin verb is not *demonstrare*, usually translated as "prove," or demonstrate in the sense of proof, but rather *probare*. Translate *probare* as prove if you like; it seems to be a correct rendering. Though the normal Latin word for probe is not probare, it makes better sense if you take Aquinas here to mean "probe": five ways of probing the meaning of God. Aquinas was somewhat skittish about saying that God "exists," and I am a lot more skittish than he was. I don't think that's the way that language about God works. It is not that God could exist and does not, but rather that it doesn't make sense to speak of him as existing. He has better things to do with his time, like cause to exist created beings that *do* exist. Except that we don't really know what it would mean to "cause to exist." Everywhere you turn in this sort of an inquiry, you come up against mysteries, and it would be wiser not to explain the wrong parts of the mystery. But we are not left speechless, as we shall see. For there are many such places in life, and some patterns run through them.

The classic example of unanswerable questions that have been mistaken by Aquinas's readers for answerable questions are just the five ways of knowing God from natural theology in Part I, Question 2, Article 3 of the *Summa Theologica*. They are in just about every anthology for beginning philosophy students, and they are usually advertised as ways to get to God using only philosophy, without faith at all. That is an appraisal that we shall question in a moment, but first look at the structure of the five ways, and treat them as about questions that *do* have answers, and see what happens when we read them in that spirit.

Anthony Kenny, in *The Five Ways*, has provided a guide to Aquinas's arguments for beginning and advanced students alike. They are often quite subtle, and Kenny supplies the background from other

## 5.4 Five Easy Pieces

texts in Aquinas and Aristotle. Each "proof" proceeds by constructing a series of causes, and then insisting that the series cannot go on forever, so there must be an initial cause, and "that is what we call God." (Kenny, p. 57.) For example, the first way, about causes of motion, insists that every moving body is moved by some other body, and the series must end in a first unmoved mover.

The five ways are modeled on Aristotle's four causes, but efficient cause appears twice, once in the first way restricted to motion, and again in the second way more generally. The third way is about material causes. For Aristotle and Aquinas that means an examination of potentiality and actuality; why do potentialities ever become actual? The fourth way is about formal causes, and shows Aquinas as almost a Platonist in quest of ideal Forms. The fifth way is about final causes, purposes, and has some kinship to design arguments.

For Aristotle, and Aquinas after him, there are four kinds of answers to why-questions, four kinds of explanations. And these five ways cover those four kinds of why-questions, four ways to ask "why?" Aquinas's account for each one is extremely brief, a short paragraph at most. Kenny shows that behind Thomas's terse summary in each case lies a topic of great subtlety, often with a complex history in other texts in Aquinas and Aristotle. The appeal to a first cause is sound (whatever may be said of other aspects of the arguments), if the world is composed of finitely many causes. The easiest way to get out of these arguments is simply to insist that the world of causes is not limited to the finite in number. Anyone who has the slightest familiarity with modern mathematics or physics will probably do just that. Kenny finds many other problems with these arguments, though I pass over them in silence here.

More seriously, something has been overlooked in Kenny's masterful treatment. The causes that Kenny tracks down as concrete instances of what Aquinas could have meant are all intra-mundane, phenomena within the world. And so the five ways, even if they were valid proofs, could only get you to yet another intra-mundane being that is the first cause in each of the four kinds of causes. Such a being would not be God, contrary to what Aquinas says in each case: "this is what we call God." So something doesn't make sense. It is normally a fallacy to change the meaning of a term in the middle of a proof; it's called the fallacy of equivocation. But here, it is *necessary* to change the meaning of the terms if we are to get to something that is *not* intra-mundane, something transcendent, something that might qualify as divine.

Other people have suspected that Aquinas didn't really intend these five ways as real proofs. David Burrell, a world-famous Thomistic scholar at the University of Notre Dame, says that his beginning students find the flaws in them quite easily, and he encourages them to do just that. Kenny has shown that they don't work very well as proofs even if you give them all benefit of the doubt that an expert in Aristotelian and medieval philosophy can give. William Placher says the five ways are not *intended* as proofs, and to read them that way is to misunderstand them. In *The Domestication of Transcendence*, he shows how to unravel the confusion. In Question 1, Thomas has already said that he is talking about God on the basis of faith. Modern students think he is talking about God on the basis of faithless philosophy in Question 2, even though Thomas never retracts what he said in Question 1 about thinking on the basis of faith. That is clue number one; these are really not meant as proofs, because they presuppose what some readers think they are meant to "prove." That's why I said it would be better to mistranslate *probare* as probe than to give it the correct rendering, prove. For a second clue, on the other side of these texts lies Question 3, supposedly about the simplicity of God. But it seems to say, in effect, that normal ways of reasoning about things in the world just don't help when we come to think about God. About things in the world, we combine and distinguish ideas, but that doesn't work for God. And that, of course, is exactly what Kenny did in his exposition of the five ways: lots of combining and distinguishing, because Kenny read these arguments in the same way that we read arguments about things in the world. For a third anomaly, many have

## 5.4 Five Easy Pieces

noticed that the first causes that are reached in each of the five ways are not necessarily God, and they are not necessarily the same *common* first cause. And for a fourth anomaly, Thomas elsewhere shows that he really doesn't have an insurmountable problem with all infinite series of causes; he accepts some (Placher, p. 25).

So what's going on when he insists on truncating *these* five series of causes? It looks as if what Thomas is showing us is that when we ask "why?" we want to come to an ending, some closure, a sense of an answer, not just more questions. To do that, you have to change what it is you are asking about; the fallacy of equivocation is *necessary*, not something to avoid. The shift occurs when we stop asking more why-questions and ask instead about the whole process of asking why-questions. He doesn't say that, of course; but we can. Thomas doesn't show that the explaining could go on forever, but he assumes it, and it is a pretty safe assumption. He truncates the series of explanations because it wouldn't be very satisfying to go on forever. Ultimately, that's not what we want when we ask why-questions. Eventually, we get tired. And so human reason, try as it may in inquiries about the world, turns to something more, something beyond. And it fails. We try to build metaphysical systems that include everything, and we always put God at the apex of the system. In the end, we fail. But it would seem that Aquinas is saying that we should expect that (Placher, p. 26–27). God remains unknowable to us, beyond what the human mind is capable of. It looks as if when we ask why-questions, in the end, we have no answers. That is a significant result.

The five ways are famous, but they are also the easy form of the problem, because they all arise in nature. At least it is possible to think they all arise in nature, to find them all in nature. And nature doesn't hurt quite the way a broken human relationship hurts. In history, we ask another kind of unanswerable question: "Why did this have to happen to me?" That question hurts more when other people are involved than when something bad just falls out of the sky. Other people hurt more than natural accidents. Mircea Eliade, in the last chapter of *Cosmos and History*, put it baldly: "The Terror of History." Growing up in the boonies, his ancestors were overrun by one empire after another, but they were never themselves the center of an empire. Instead, they were starved, brutalized, marginalized, always on the outside looking in. The really hard problems are in human living, not with nature but with history. When we began with exposure, limitation, and need, we began with the hardest of human problems. We have said already that there is no answer to "why embrace exposure, limitation, and need as blessing-bearing?" It is time to look a little more at unanswerable why-questions, going beyond what Aquinas does in his five ways. The five ways, after all, are barely a prologue to what follows.

## 5.5 Unanswerable Questions

Consider the possibility that the word 'God' is not a word that refers to a being, something that might or might not exist. Not because God necessarily has to exist, for which there are good arguments, if you get to make some assumptions and customize the meaning of "exist." Rather it doesn't *make sense* to say that God exists. Nor does it make sense to say that He does not exist. "God exists" is not how the concept of God works. "God exists" does not even rise to the level of falsehood. If God does not exist, he does, however, cause to exist created beings that do exist. That's how the concept of God works. That's what he does. This God does not need to exist in order to act.

This is a start, but it still doesn't really get us far enough. Another possibility, more interesting and only a little different, is that the term 'God' does not refer to anything at all, because it is a place-marker in language for the missing answers to all these unanswerable questions. It doesn't refer to a being or a cause, but it does enable us to deal with these unanswerable questions. There are many situations in life when we ask unanswerable questions, from "Why did this happen to me?" to "Why is the cosmos orderly?" to "Why do exposure, limitation, and need do us any good?" The term 'God' allows us to talk about all these

## 5.5 Unanswerable Questions

situations at once. The term 'God' allows us to say something about real reality, the part of reality that we bump into when we come to an unanswerable question. The term 'God' allows us to tell it like it is, it allows us to acknowledge the way things are, it discloses how things are with us. We are not just talking about ourselves when we use the term 'God,' though some people may think we are. They might ask, in frustration, if you aren't just talking about yourselves and your own experience, then what *are* you talking about? The term 'God' *must* refer to *something*. But it doesn't. The claim that it must is just an argument by tantrum. Language doesn't always work that way. And that doesn't mean that the language of God is just about ourselves; it is about the world, the world we live in, it is very much about the way things are with us.

When you come up against an unanswerable question, there are several ways you can go. You can ignore it. If other people pester you with unanswerable questions, you can deny them. You can treat them as answerable questions, and this is usually the most effective strategy to hide your situation and make the real question invisible. But if you do treat an unanswerable question as answerable, that usually means you have changed the meaning of the question. If you can't ignore the question and won't deny it, you can just sit there and feel slightly uncomfortable. You may be in anguish, you may be in gratitude (remember Turkey Day, in *Waters*?). There is more in the last option than meets the eye.

Or, in another sort of situation, when you step back and think about your knowledge of the world, and you see how much of it depends on human interpretation, you can almost panic. You only get answers to questions that you actually ask—and those questions are all of human making. So in a real sense, all your knowledge depends on the human invention of your questions. Are the answers in any sense true? Well, yes. But do they tell you how things are *apart from your questions*? No. That's when the temptation to panic sets in. It's easily remedied by television, or a snack, or other people. But it's there nevertheless.

This is chaos. We shall come to this chaos again shortly, when we look at what happens when people pray.

If we cannot see answers to our unanswerable questions, we *can* see the questions, and we can see how those questions arise in life. That's the next place to look. What does it mean to ask *why*? It means tell me how my world works, tell me how my life fits into the world. Tell me how to make sense of my life in the world. Give me reasons, give me a narrative into which I fit, a narrative in which I can be at home. Make the world a home for me. (That was Edward Hobbs's definition of theology, by the way.)

I want to know how the world fits together, and in the background are the possibilities for living for me and my friends and neighbors. I want to know how things work, what we can do with them, what other people have already done with them, what the consequences are, what their motives are. Ultimately, these are interactional and existential questions, not theoretical questions. I am being-in-the-world, to use Martin Heidegger's phrase, and I want to know.

When we ask what looks like a theoretical question, such as what's going on in the Orion Nebula, we want more than just a theory of stellar evolution. The beauty of deep-space photographs is a clue, but only a clue. We look out on the formation of new stars in the Orion Nebula, and we see where our sun came from. The sun that gives us light and warmth, the sun at the center of a stable planetary system. When we look at the Ring Nebula in Lyra, we see the remains after a star has exploded. Stars are *big*, they don't last forever, when they die they blow up, and the explosions are bigger than our entire solar system. This is our world: we are fortunate enough to live on a balmy rock at the bottom of a transparent atmosphere, so we can see out, and when we look out, what we see touches us in the heart. For we know that if a star did something like that anywhere close to us, we would be toast. We feel very small, and we feel very privileged. To ask why is to ask how we fit into the world.

Harder than questions in the natural sciences are why me, why pain, why can't so-and-so be reasonable, why broken human relationships? Why must I die, why limitation, why do I have to lose those I love? Why did this have to happen to me? That's where the rubber hits the road and leaves skid-marks. Always at stake are things that bestow life and impose death. Sometimes a little bit at a time, sometimes not so little.

What bestows life or imposes death: call it a "bloid." Is there a big Bloid behind all the little bloids? That depends on how you view things. Bloid is one functional definition of deity. If there are many bloids, with no unity in them, the world is polytheistic. If there is unity and coherence, one prerequisite for radical monotheism is met; but only one.

Usually, we don't really know what will bestow life or impose death, beyond a few simple things, how not to get burned by the stove, how to get the soufflé to rise. We would always like to know more. To ask to know the bloids is to ask for a kind of control, conceptual control even if not practical control. We ask to be let out of anxiety, out of finitude, out of creaturehood. You might think that to ask out of creaturehood is always sinful, but things are not so obvious. It can also be to offer up our creaturehood to the almighty Void that we cannot see. Even Jesus prayed, "let this cup pass from me." We could just as well ask of God, "We wish you were not so holy, a little less mysterious, a little more objective, a little more comforting. We wish you were just a little more substantial, so we could see you. Almighty Nothing, you're making us nervous." But what we want is not given to us.

## 5.6  Analogies

Look at how another age handled the problem. Aristotelians in theology (Thomas Aquinas and his latter-day students) distinguish between a science's own proper questions and its presuppositions. A science cannot demonstrate its own presuppositions; to do so would be sort of like digging up the ground you are standing on. Those presuppositions have to come from some other science, or from faith. When you are assuming that the cosmos is orderly and intelligible (and you have to assume that to do science), you are making an assumption on faith. You don't know ahead of time how the order will turn out. You just trust that it will come out in the wash, somehow. (Some scientific problems wait centuries for a solution. Patience is necessary.) This is very much a case of trusting in limitation, by the way. You don't know ahead of time what the limitations of the natural world are, you do trust that they are there, and you do trust that you can find some good in them when you try to understand them.

When you trace presuppositions back, sooner or later, you run out of answers (or just run out of energy), and there you come to the starting point of faith. It may be "revelation," or natural theology, or other things, just the weight of experience. You have bumped into presuppositions that come from faith, but their roots in faith are not recognized. If you then take the Five Ways as real proofs, you would miss the fact that they are places where you meet a certain kind of unanswerable question.

Yet the Thomists were not born yesterday; they know which way is up. Their chosen explanation goes by the deceptively simple name of "analogy." And if you play by the rules, it works. Analogy is a device to speak of transcendence without compromising it, without domesticating it. Analogy happens when we see one part of life in the light of another. (That's my definition, not the standard Thomistic definition, but it works.) What happens next is that you take an experience from within human life, within the world, and use it to make sense of unanswerable questions.

Well, what is analogy? There is a scene in one of C. S. Lewis's Narnia stories, *The Silver Chair*, in which our protagonists, Jill and Eustace and Puddleglum, are held captive underground by a Witch. The Witch represents the evil forces of secularism, and more particularly, the atheist philosophers who were Lewis's neighbors at Oxford.

## 5.6 Analogies

It looks like our heroes will never get out. In fact, the Witch is trying to tell them that there really *isn't* a world of light above ground; this underground cave world is all there is. (Lewis is pulling your leg in more ways than just one, for those of you who have read Plato; and he was nothing if not a Platonist.) The Witch deconstructs all their protests as mere imagination, mere projections, mere analogies, and childish ones at that. Jill and Eustace protest that they were sent by Aslan, the Lion, and they have lived where the sun rises and sets every day. She doesn't believe in lions or a world above-ground, and defies them to exhibit any proof of it for her. They point to the lamp and her cat, and say that the sun is like the lamp, but bigger, and Aslan is like her cat, but bigger. But she says they are just imagining things. Only lamps and cats are real; Lions and suns are just imagination. (She puts out smoke, too, from the fire in the fireplace, and the magical smoke is putting them to sleep, and they start to believe her.)

So how *do* you come to have an idea of God? Is it like the Witch says, only lamps and cats are real, but not suns and Lions? Everyday truths and a few everyday good people, but there is no transcendent truth, and there is no transcendent source of good, that shows itself in the world and sets things right?

Lewis's answer is not my answer, and I record this fact despite the deepest gratitude to him. My grandfather bought these stories for me, one by one, as they were published in the 1950s, during the years I was learning to read. They are among the first books I remember, and they inspired my heart as well as informed my mind. (In the beginning were the Narnia stories!) They are designed to show what it feels like to be a Christian, not just to convey information. They are meant for the heart and lungs, for vigor and exhilaration, not for the head and careful reason.

But Lewis was a Platonist, and I am not. If you look again at the encounter between the Witch and Jill, Eustace, and Puddleglum, there is more there than Lewis knew. First, they escape from the Witch's induced illusions when Puddleglum stamps the fire out—and burns his feet badly in the process, replacing the sweet smell of magic with the harsh and painful smell of burned flesh. It costs suffering to penetrate the illusions that would abolish transcendence. (Exposure, limitation, and need are the place in life where we see transcendence when we see blessing in them.) So far, so good. Here, Lewis is right, and his instincts are on the Way of the Cross. But look again. The Witch is in effect saying to the children, for she is the voice of atheist scoffers in the twentieth century (they called themselves Logical Positivists in Lewis's day), "your religious ideas are just analogies." They take the bait—as Platonists must, and Lewis did—and answer that no, suns and Lions are real, implicitly in the same way that lamps and cats are real. For of course, in the Narnia stories, they *were* real in the same way. But the Narnia stories do have a larger context, one in mid-twentieth century English-speaking academia (remember "Tickets to Bali H'ai," in *Waters*?), and it is to that audience that they speak.

*Just* analogies? Whenever someone says that *A* is "just" *B*, what he really means, implicitly, is that *A* is *not C*. He may not know what *C* would be, he may not want you to know or even imagine. He may be lazy. But whenever the word "just" appears in this way, there is always something lurking in the background. What is in the background here is the assumption that analogies cannot really speak truth. Analogies are not allowed to say anything about the human condition, are not allowed to tell us how things really are. And that is clearly false—whether Lewis realized it or not—because the Narnia stories are themselves analogies. They are fiction, and they are also true. How can that be? How does language work, that fiction can be true? (Or *Life of Brian*, a parody of the Gospels? Or the Gospels, as parodies of the Exodus? Remember, in *Waters*, section 8.3, "Darmok at Tanagra"?)

The Platonist solution to the children's problem, and the problem of Christianity in the modern world, is to insist on the simple reality of the transcendent world and its inhabitants. I would like to try another approach. On my own testimony elsewhere, I have no business trying

## 5.6 Analogies

to kick Platonists out of the Church, and that is certainly not my intention, despite the fact that I suspect people of using Platonism and the supernatural as a cover for theologically dubious projects. Probably mostly Christians in the West have been Platonists, and on any generous view, most of them are in heaven. But some people don't find Platonism very helpful, and another approach may work better.

Can analogy work better? And why is it so easily confused? Remember that C. S. Lewis was trying to fend off the hecklers at Oxford and Cambridge, and claim some reality for Christian images, Christian terms, Christian language, Christian life. Notice first that there are multiple analogies in the story. Aslan, the lion, is an analogy for Christ, and the underground/above ground contrast is an analogy both for Plato's Myth of the Cave and for the dualist cosmos that some Christians would like to live in. But the story itself, the story of lamps and cats and suns and lions, is an analogy for understanding the world of Britain and twentieth-century philosophy. *Within* the story, of course, suns and lions exist every bit in the same way as lamps and cats. Therein lies the snare: for if you transfer the story to real life simply, then your language is univocal and not analogical. Then the term 'God' has to refer to a being, one that might or might not exist. But if you treat the language of God as analogical, then things are different. You can make sense of unanswerable questions in life in terms of, by analogy with, answerable questions, ordinary parts of life. You can use happy family life as the analogy for ultimate reality. But that is your *choice*.

If you forget what you are doing, you will turn transcendence into an object, and then suck that object into the world. That is called domesticating transcendence. (See Placher, 1996.) But if you remember what you are doing, you can enjoy transcendence without compromising it. You can see the untamed chaos in the cosmos, and not be destroyed by it. You can be fascinated and enchanted, and you can live with your anxieties. If you forget what you are doing, you will see only your own imaginations, and you will not know that they are a product of your own mind. What you see will not be ultimate reality, nor will it be transcendent. But if you remember what you are doing, you can look on the face of chaos and live. (This was called the Fear of the Lord in the Common Documents.)

The best way to see how to safeguard these analogies is to look at how to break them. When the name "God" was turned too easily into the name of a being, we substituted "The Way Things Are." But that, too, can be broken, and the next thing to do is to see how. Only then can we look at what happens when we approach TWTA and speak to it as to a person.

## 5.7 How To Break Anything

Look at how the language of biblical religion so easily gets mistreated. How do you break the language of transcendence? Breaking happens when we forget that "The Way Things Are" was the answer to some questions, namely, "Why embrace all of life as good, even its hard and painful parts?" and "Why take human life as essentially historical?" (The historical part was in *Waters*; here we focus on the pains.) There are two ways to forget that "the way things are" is the answer to a question. One way is metaphysical, and the other way is practical or moral. In the metaphysical option, "the way things are" becomes a description of the world or of ultimate reality or of "Being" or of some such abstraction. In the moral way, you forget that each person has to answer the question for himself. The rightness of embracing human life in this historical world as good is not something objective, from which human commitment can be removed. It is intensely practical, and it cannot be demonstrated to skeptics.

If you forget that TWTA is the answer to a question, then you can mistake it for a description, for a term that refers to something. Even as the answer to a question, it doesn't tell you much. Certainly not much about how the cosmos is, though it tells you a great deal about human life in the cosmos. It's the beginning of how to live. It tells you

## 5.7 How To Break Anything

that you are blessed, even though you can't see anyone or anything transcendent who has blessed you.

Look at the metaphysical way of forgetting first. This works by treating all nouns as if they refer to something. That's an instinct that appeals to everybody in the Western tradition. Every noun refers to something, and what it refers to exists someplace. Simply. Without difficulties. I am not being entirely fair, but also not entirely unfair.

What happens when you go down this road? First, transcendence gets "domesticated," tamed. The chaos of the universe becomes invisible, and that makes a lot of discomfort go away. Here, ultimate reality is never really an enemy; it is originally a friend. Soon, you are on the way to getting out of exposure, limitation, and need, because the God will save you from them by getting you out of them. Or, if the pains of life are still seen, you can get out of this life to get out of its pains. Or, in another variation on Platonism in theology, if you take the unanswerable questions as answerable ones, the answers you get tend to be naturalistic.

If TWTA is *just* a description of the world, you are on your way to pantheism, the idea that the world *itself* is divine, is god. That's nice, but it's not biblical religion. In desperation, or for lack of logic or imagination, even some Christian theologians do things like this.

Suppose the term TWTA means something unknowable but still not the world itself, then what? God becomes Being, Being-itself, mysterious, but still some*thing*. In one version, the world (and especially people in it) are then made of the same god-stuff as this original mysterious reality. The world "emanates" from that mysterious Being. There are a lot of problems here. In the first place, emanation and creation are not the same thing. In creation, the created order is *not* made of god-stuff, it is different. That's true no matter how much some parts of it may be made in the image of God. If humans are made of God-stuff, not radically different from the deity, then the problem of human sin more or less goes away. People are not really sinners after all, and there's no reason to feel guilty for anything. All your problems come from forgetting that you are made of god-stuff. That way lies more than just Neoplatonism; that way lies Gnosticism, if you go far enough. Gnosticism is a story for another time, but for now, it's enough to say that it's not the same thing as biblical religion.

If you don't want to go all the way to Gnosticism, you can stop with mysticism, and just meditate your way into happiness and peace with the cosmos. Sometimes this gets called the "Perennial Philosophy," meaning the thesis that at bottom all religions are really the same, they are all just about meditation and peace. A casual familiarity with texts from the world's religions, beautiful as they all are, will convince any candid reader that they are not all the same. They are not all doing the same thing. But the Perennial Philosophy claims that they *should* be, or that "deep down," they are. It can get away with this claim because most religions do spend some time focusing on activities devoted to recognition and intention—often meditation of some sort. Overlooked is the fact that different religions recognize and intend quite different things with their lives. Some versions of the Perennial Philosophy have found a home in most of the world's religions, but that doesn't make it the heart of any religion but itself. The people who do the Perennial Philosophy report that they are happy; I won't deny them that. But to note only the most salient differences from biblical religion, the Perennial Philosophy doesn't care much about history, and it doesn't deal with the pains of life in quite the way that a historical religion does.

What about the practical and moral way of forgetting that The Way Things Are is the answer to a question? It is very much about the world, but it is also always a commitment; it is not a claim about the world from which its claimers can dodge responsibility.

Look at how the commitment works. It is a personal commitment, but it is not an *individual* commitment. It is a personal commitment made in community, never alone. It is a way of living, and it asserts, as all human acts do, that it is the right way to live. It is not subjective, mere caprice, whimsy, or taste. As a way of living that implicitly

## 5.7 How To Break Anything

asserts its own rightness, it makes a claim on other people by its example. It is not objective in the sense of objectivation in the natural sciences: there, objects have been stripped of all human involvements. Here, it is the human involvements themselves that challenge by their example.

See what happens if you mistake this claim for something "objective." Things get ugly real fast. You can now tell someone else, "your pains bring you good, and you should embrace them as good." The least of the problems is that such a stance opens the way to oppression. Worse than the fate of the victims is that of the oppressors. For you are in the position of the man in the epistle of James who said to the poor, "I wish you well, keep yourself warm and eat plenty" (2.16), without doing anything to help. The one who forgets his own commitment in saying that the right thing to do is to embrace others' need and limitation can now stiff the poor and impose limitation on those he does not like. The one who forgets his own commitment has forgotten that "the way things are" applies to himself before it could ever apply to anyone else.

What, then, can people of this faith say to outsiders and to those who suffer? We come to that in more detail in sections 7.2 and 7.3. For now, the model is a variation on the great Deuteronomic sermon in the end of Joshua, and it is a question: "Whom will you serve?" There is no *proof* that one way is better than another, no proof apart from living, no proof that would or could convince those who choose differently. What can one say? Toward those who do not believe that embracing the pains of life as part of a good life is the way things are, we say, "We'll do what we can to relieve your suffering, even to share in it, because whether or not you find good in your life, we do. But we won't support you in your denial of the goodness of life." That may not be entirely welcome, especially when the others are not in serious suffering but instead are merely trying to evade the blessings in more modest pains of life. This way of speaking certainly poses a challenge, but it is not the bad faith of the man in the epistle of James. Toward those who are too overwhelmed in suffering and affliction to even think about the goodness of life, appropriate help is usually welcome. Other things can wait.

In a strange way, ultimate reality, what *is*, is a matter of choice, and it is still a reality apart from human choices. This looks like a paradox, but I think it is just an idea that Western languages have made impossible to state clearly. This is a puzzle that the Western tradition has not been able to handle at all well. That's why people are so easily tempted to forget that "the way things are" is the answer to a question, and an answer that comes from human commitment, not some non-human objective reality. The Western tradition's language was designed to enforce responsibility against the sophists (today we call them deconstructionists), but it easily becomes a tool to gain power over anything, even the language of God. And if you can break the language of God, you can break anything.

## 5.8 Bag Lady

We have all seen her: in the squalor of an inner-city street, beside vacant lots full of gravel, weeds, broken bottles, trash on one side and shabby buildings way overdue for maintenance on the other, there comes a bag lady pushing a shopping cart with all her worldly possessions in it. She's not in very good shape. And she is talking, but there is no one she's talking to. That's what's frightening: she's carrying on one half of a conversation, but there's nobody for the other half. After you check to make sure she's not on a cell-phone (upscale bag ladies, these days!), then you feel creepy. And if the bag lady is actually a man, you are a little nervous for your safety, because someone who talks to nobody could be dangerous. The conversation is usually fairly intense; the bag lady is in some pain, she has grievances, she is complaining.

Have you listened to the Great Bag Lady of History? As She talks to the Lord of History? Lately?

## 5.8 Bag Lady

> Surely, for your sake have I suffered reproach,
> and shame has covered my face.
>
> I have become a stranger to my own kindred,
> an alien to my mother's children.
>
> Zeal for your house has eaten me up;
> the scorn of those who scorn you has fallen upon me.
>
> I humbled myself with fasting,
> but that was turned to my reproach.
>
> I put on sack-cloth also,
> and became a byword among them.
>
> Those who sit at the gate murmur against me,
> and the drunkards make songs about me.

My neighbors are picking on me, I tried to be faithful to you, but they think I'm dying, and they plan to take away what little I have, even before I'm dead. When the bag lady on the street is giving thanks, you don't hear it; today's bag ladies would be embarrassed to give thanks in public to Mr. Not-There. Often, with thanks, we are speechless. But the Psalms give thanks, thanks aplenty. Sometimes she sings:

> I called to the LORD in my distress;
> the LORD answered by setting me free.
>
> The LORD is at my side, therefore I will not fear;
> what can anyone do to me? . . .
>
> This is the LORD's doing,
> and it is marvelous in our eyes.

> On this day the LORD has acted;
> we will rejoice and be glad in it.
>
> Blessed is he who comes in the name of the Lord;
> we bless you from the house of the LORD.

Prayer is like the bag lady. Talking to God is like the bag lady talking to whoever it is she talks to. He's not there. ("I shall be with you as who I am shall I be with you," as was heard from the Burning Bush?)

Nothing will save you, so trust in nothing? You thought you just heard me say trust in nothing, i.e., *dis*trust everything. That's not what the text says: it says *trust* in nothing, and it means what it says. Trust in nothing is quite different from distrust in everything, which is what people usually hear. Trust, not distrust. The text means what it says: *trust* in nothing, trust in *the* nothing, trust in *this* nothing. Nothing loves you, so love your neighbor as one like yourself? Nothing will expose you, so it's time to repent, the jig is up? Nothing cares about you, so you treat your body as a temple of the Holy Spirit?

Almighty Nothing, Father of all mercies, we do give you our humble and hearty thanks? We come to you, Lord Nothing, with praise and thanksgiving, through Jesus Christ your Son? Holy and Gracious Nothing, in your infinite love, you made us for yourself?! Not even Monty Python could have attempted something like that.

But of course, where I have garbled the texts, they usually read *Father*. That is, we have been enabled to call this almighty Void, this Nothing that will save us, "Father." A certain amount of dread is inevitable at this point. When you can be like the bag lady, when you can talk to the nothing, then you can pray in a way that was not possible before.

When you do start talking to the nothing, you are putting yourself on the line. You are out there all alone. Just like the bag lady. You are committed—if promises actually work, if the language of promises actually works. You are committed to embracing life in history, in full view of all its pains, as good, as a blessing. (At least you are, if you start talking to *this* nothing. There are many nothings, and they are not all the same.) You know that you will be destroyed in the end, and you have given thanks. As John Michael Murphy once said in a sonnet entitled "Lent,"

> Face it, old truant, this dark disease in your veins
> You handle by dying. Life's what you get for your pains.

Exposure, limitation, and need call you, choose you, save you; you do not choose them.

But how else could you commit yourself *as a person*, than by talking as a person to another person? Even when the Other is not there? Almighty Nothing may come to us as three prosopons, but that does not make it a person. We are persons. That is why we have to relate to it as persons. How else could you put your life on the line?

Why do we see ultimate reality in the light of our own interpersonal relationships? (But how else could we see it?)

## 5.9  I Am Not Making This Up

It could appear as if we have said that God does not exist. The appearance is correct. A better statement might go something like this:

> God does not exist, God causes to exist created beings
> that do exist; God does not need to exist in order to act.

To be fussy, God does not exist not because he could exist and does not, but because existing is not how God and the concept of God work. There are quite sensible things that can be said of God and disagreed about, but so far as I can see, existence is not one of them. And to be fully candid, The second clause of the sentence set off above would be a highly analogical use of the word "cause." If it marks the missing answers to unanswerable why-questions, it works not so much like causes but in place of causes.

It may come as a surprise that treating God as not "existing" is not new, *in Christian theology*. The reader is entitled to some warrant for this claim, and so this section is in a sense one long footnote, a guide to a few places in the literature where philosophical theologians understand God as something other than an entity that exists, a "supreme being," in the language of the modern world. Those who don't like footnotes can happily skip it. It won't even be a complete footnote, with all the places in the history of Christian philosophy where people have realized that God doesn't make sense as a being among other beings.

In biblical times, these questions did not arise. People used the inherited language, and it did not occur to them to talk about the "existence" of God. Psalm 14 as it is commonly translated opens with "The fool has said in his heart, there is no God." Some who know Hebrew better than I do tell me that it should be understood as, "The fool has said in his heart, to God, No!" This is practical atheism, it is not about the "existence" of God. And even if it were, it would be virtually unique in the Common Documents. Those documents don't worry about existence. The New Testament is no different, and I don't think the Talmuds are either. In the biblical tradition you could have said this is just the way we talk about life. But there was not much interest in asking about the existence of God, and less interest in "being" as an abstract concept. Being is an Indo-European philosophical problem, and in Israelite religion, the god(s) simply designate different ways of living. That sounds much more subjective than it really was: They are about competing realities, and those realities are very active in human life and the world. You can see them at work. And they are in conflict; one can win against another. But to ask whether they "exist" was not a sensible question.

How language works is a thoroughly modern question. Biblical writers did not worry about it, they just took their language for granted. We have to worry about it, because we can no longer take our own

## 5.9 I Am Not Making This Up

inherited language for granted. It is we who listen to our inherited language, and notice that it doesn't work the way we thought it did. So we have to ask how our language works and what it does for us.

The existence of God began to be a problem when Christian theologians learned Greek philosophy, and even then, it took a few centuries for the problem to show itself. The problem is older, and more general, in Greek philosophy itself, before any Greeks became Christians. There is an out-of-print but very good history by an Australian, Raoul Mortley. It is called *From Word to Silence*, and its two volumes are entitled *The Rise and Fall of Logos* and *The Way of Negation, Christian and Greek*. The title of the first volume tells the thesis. The story starts before Plato, with confidence that human reason (*logos*, also language) can find answers to the basic questions of life. That confidence in the all-powerful capacities of language is dashed in the end. Another strategy unfolds over the succeeding twelve centuries, and it is called the way of negation. If we can't tell what some things are, perhaps we can tell what they are not.

The most famous and most read Christian example of this approach is known only by his pen-name, Dionysius. He pretended to be the Dionysius the Areopagite of Acts 17.34. That was enough to make sure people read him carefully. But his writing makes more sense coming from the fifth or sixth century than from the first, for he knows Neoplatonic philosophers of the fifth century and he is quoted early in the sixth century. Today, he is usually known as Pseudo-Dionysius. Pseudo-Dionysius stands at the crossroads of a mystical tradition in Christianity, one that turned from thinking of God unreflectively in language that makes him sound like a being to thinking of God as a mystery. "He will not come to be. No. He is not. Rather, he is the essence of being for the things which have being" (*The Divine Names*, 817d, chapter 5, section 4, p. 98 of the Luibheid translation.) Dionysius goes on at great length to show how God, even though he is not an existing being, nevertheless stands at the head of the hierarchy of being and beings. That is the way of philosophy. First, some others in the tradition. Let me come to Thomas Aquinas last, because he leaves us a short meditation that is in some ways the most interesting.

One who followed Dionysius was John of Damascus, about a century later. He says of God,

> For He does not belong to the number of beings, not because He does not exist, but because he transcends all beings and being itself. And if knowledge respects beings, then that which transcends knowledge will certainly transcend essence, and, conversely, what transcends essence will transcend knowledge. (*The Orthodox Faith*, Book I, ch. 4; p. 172 of the Chase translation.)

William Placher quotes this (Placher, p. 10). John of Damascus passes on the problem from Pseudo-Dionysius; Thomas Aquinas will pick it up in these terms. John Damascene, as is apparent, waffles, as most in this tradition do, when it comes to saying whether God "exists" or not; but those who waffle have to equivocate on the meanings of "exist." I would rather not equivocate on the meanings of that word, in order to make a point that can't be made as well in any other way.

Paul Tillich dismissed God as a being among other beings, but had great interest in God as ultimate reality (*Systematic Theology*, 1:235). A few pages earlier, he defined the gods as the source of meaning in life, rather than as personified beings. What makes human life meaningful or good is not originally a question about the existence of any beings, and it certainly can be answered favorably without postulating the existence of God as a being among other beings. In passing, Tillich's move to identify God with Being itself (not a move that I would make) has precedent in Pseudo-Dionysius.

Theologians who have read Martin Heidegger generally follow a similar path. John Macquarrie (1966, pp. 105 ff.) denies that God and being are simply synonymous; *being* is a neutral term, but to call something God is to speak with faith, with commitment. Yet God is, if not being simply, nevertheless *holy* being. God is most certainly not *a* being.

## 5.9 I Am Not Making This Up

> The assertion "god exists" is not to be taken as meaning that there is to be found a being possessing such and such characteristics. "God exists" is a way of asserting what would perhaps be more exactly expressed as the holiness of being. But it is precisely the assertion of the holiness of being that is denied by atheism. . . . (p. 109).

"$X$ does not exist" can mean that it could exist (but does not), or it can mean that existence is not how the concept of $X$ works. Here, the contrast to existence is not non-existence but holiness.

The question, then, is about the goodness of a world that is not ultimately friendly. It destroys us in the end. Can such a world have anything holy behind it? It is most certainly not the world that is God; but can anything be God?

Modern theologians have written this way, often without much attention to Dionysius at all. H. Richard Niebuhr spoke of God as "only the 'void' out of which everything comes and to which everything returns." We first saw this meditation on disaster and hope in section 5.2, p. 54 above. For Niebuhr, the ultimate question in life is whether to trust that void. Without offering any of the comforts of a God that "exists," he merely observes that people do trust in that void. Niebuhr is typical of the twentieth-century Neo-Orthodox, and in a distant way, typical also of the existentialists (if anything could be called typical of them). He was influenced by (among many others) Rudolf Bultmann and Martin Heidegger, but I would conjecture even more influenced by his inheritance from John Calvin. It is worth noting in passing that Niebuhr follows the Neoplatonists when he says that we come from and return to the Void that is the source and end of all being.

Gregory Rocca (1993, pp. 648-649) wrote about the *via negativa* and its place in Christian theology, with special attention to Thomas Aquinas. He meditated on a lucid passage in Saint Thomas's commentary on Peter Lombard's *Sentences*, *Super Sententiarum* 1.8.1.1 ad 4. This passage comes from an inquiry about being and God, asking whether "being" is properly said of God. After the objections (there are four of them), Thomas cites Exodus 3.14, which in his translation was "ego sum qui sum," I am who I am. This is in answer to Moses' question at the burning bush, "What is your name?" Ego sum qui sum, I am who I am. As Thomas meditates on these words, even in a dumbed-down Indo-European translation, they convey something of the awesome mystery that John Courtney Murray found in the Hebrew, "eyeh asher eyeh," "I shall be with you as who I am shall I be with you." But in the Latin, it looks like the name of God is "qui sum," Who I am, and that is what the tradition has already wrestled with before Aquinas came to the problem.

Here are the objections, taken very loosely: (1) The name of God should be peculiar to God alone, and being (*esse*) applies to pretty much everything. (2) We can only speak of God as we know God, and John of Damascus has said that we can't know much about God. (3) created wisdom is insufficient to the task of naming God. (4) John of Damascus said in *The Orthodox Faith* that "qui est" doesn't tell us what God is, it just indicates a certain depth, infinite of substance. (Actually, he says it is a *pelagus*, an ocean of infinity, an abyss. This may be where Rocca got the title for his own meditations on the problem.) But we can't understand infinity, so "qui est" (or "qui sum") is not a viable name of God. Thomas replies that, contrary to the objections, far from being unusable, "qui sum" is the most proper of all names of God. Along the way, he notes that John of Damascus has said that "qui est" does not apply only to determinate or particular things, but that here we can use it only by negation. He also footnotes Pseudo-Dionysius and Avicenna; that pretty much covers the bases in the tradition.

When the reply to the fourth objection comes, Thomas invokes Damascene to explain his own writing: To be sure, "qui est" is here not particular in its application, but it also has to be viewed as a negation and not something positive. Here is the body of the answer, in Rocca's translation:

> When we proceed into God through the way of negation [*via remotionis*, not *via negationis*], first we deny of him

## 5.9 I Am Not Making This Up

> all corporeal things [or corporeal realities]; and next, we even deny intellectual things as they are found in creatures, like goodness and wisdom, and then there remains in our understanding only the fact that God exists, and nothing further, so that it suffers a kind of confusion.

Exactly. The fact that God exists is "quia est"—in English, it would a play on "qui est"; in Latin it may or may not be. And so by stages the translation into Indo-European languages fascinated with Being has torn from the mystery of holy non-existence a tiny crumb of existence to console the desolate soul. There's not much in "I will be who I will be," but philosophy will make do with what it has to work with, especially in translation. Aquinas continues (p. 67 of the Parma edition):

> Lastly, however, we even remove from him his very existence, as it is in creatures, and then our understanding remains in a certain darkness of ignorance [*tenebra ignorantiae*] according to which, as Dionysius says, we are best united to God in this present state of life; and this is a sort of thick darkness [*caligo*] in which God is said to dwell. (Rocca, pp. 648–649.)

*Caligo* means thick fog. Sort of reminds you of the beginning of Ezekiel, when Ezekiel saw the deity hovering over the northern Mesopotamian plains, doesn't it? The space-alien bodyguards wheeling in all directions around the thick glowing cloud that hides the mystery of God? Aquinas and Rocca stand in a very old tradition.

If it goes back deep into the Bible, in philosophical terms it appears only in late antiquity, with Pseudo-Dionysius and perhaps others. When God is observed not to be a being among other beings, theologians generally pursue the matter in the direction of the mystery of being. After all, the text in Exodus 3.14 sounds, especially in translation, like it is about being, being in the abstract, being as a mystery. That is, the theologians have become philosophers. As they wonder out loud, their non-existent God sounds more and more like a being that exists. What was denied in the "negative way" creeps back in what can nevertheless still be said about God. Thus does philosophy gratify the cravings of the heart when it must.

Another possibility and one less explored than philosophy would be to look at the history of covenant, to think historically, theologically, and covenantally before coming to philosophy. When people have asked themselves why they wished to affirm human life in this historical world and answered with something like "because that's the way things are," they lived in particular circumstances in particular times and places. They merely trusted that the future would bring blessing as the past had; that's what covenant means. What it meant to live in history has not always been the same in every age. What it meant to affirm human life in face of its pains was not always the same. That much can be seen just by looking at the Bible: in the beginning, in the Exodus, things are sunny and upbeat. The Exodus is almost like a romantic action movie. Almost. But when the Assyrians and Babylonians came, it looked like disaster would never be remedied, and indeed some features of life before the Exile were never restored. One age wants children and mere survival in peace; another wants help against its tribal enemies; another has to deal with mortality; yet another wants forgiveness of sins, justification; another still just wants simple meaning in life instead of meaninglessness. All have lived within the biblical tradition.

So the question, "why live this way?" changes its meaning over the course of centuries. Whether questions about Being are sensible or not, I don't know. Probably they are, but they would require sifting through an enormous history of philosophy. The question of covenant will persist as long as people choose a historical-covenantal religion. I am inclined to leave well enough alone, and not claim that there exists a being within the thick darkness that human reason cannot penetrate. Nor am I comfortable in following those who reason philosophically about that thick darkness. What we cannot know, we cannot talk about

## 5.9 I Am Not Making This Up

as if we knew it. That does not make God's acts in the world less real. In our frustration with negative theology, we cry out:

> Almighty Nothing, why can't you just exist, why can't you give us a little something to know, a little comfort? Why must you be so holy?

Almighty Nothing just smiles. We ask, with Moses, "Who *are* you?" Almighty Nothing just tells us to put one foot in front of the other and get back to dealing with this world. Be content with today's bread for today, and wait until tomorrow before worrying about bread for tomorrow. Moses was told to get back to Egypt so he could get out of nature and into history. That is our task, too: to live in history with trust, faith, hope, and love. But it is easy to see why we so crave the beatific vision! And we can see why, as John Courtney Murray observed, the Hebrews in the Exodus constantly asked whether God would be "with them." A God who does not need to exist in order to act will make people acutely anxious.

Gregory Rocca observed that the *via negativa* or negative way in theology works only because it is set within the larger framework of positive assertions about God. I think this is absolutely necessary: no one could ever undertake the terrors of negative theology without the assurances of something positive beforehand. That something positive usually comes in the form of a contagious faith that has been caught from other people. Even the Hebrews in the wilderness looked back on the interview at the burning bush only in light of their marvelous escape from Egypt; faith begins in a surplus of gratitude, as we saw in *Waters*. We reason about faith as members of the Great Bag Lady of History or not at all. The larger positive framework is simply the affirmation of human life in this historical world as good and as blessed. My impression of the article in which Rocca speaks of "hovering over the abyss" is that, like Thomas, Dionysius, and the tradition that runs through them, he can sustain negative philosophical claims about God because of prior positive theological claims about

God. My preference is to root theology in the soil of history and covenant instead of building it on a foundation in philosophy. Perhaps Thomas could not do that, but today we can. Thomas's problem was Aristotle, but our problem is history. The way of history and covenant leaves us with a darker darkness and a thicker fog than the way of philosophy does. Nevertheless, by now, thirty-odd centuries on, philosophy is part of the history of covenant, and we learn greatly from philosophy. It was philosophy that illuminated for us the thick darkness around God. Rather than try to penetrate that thick darkness, we simply affirm human life in history as good, as blessed, but we don't know in advance *how* it will be good. We merely trust that the future will reward this trust as the past has. If trust is not naive, it knows that its reward will often not be painless.

# Chapter 6
# Here With Us

## 6.1 Children's Games

Think back on that time when, as children, you concocted a game, made up the moves and the rules, and then invited your parents to play. If not parents, whatever big people were around and available. The adults enter into the game with almost a straight face, and the children are happy. (In fact, the children are not just happy, they are enchanted.) Their made-up world is now real, and they have a sense of blessing. In a slightly different form of the experience, and years later on, as adults, children asked us to play. We were the ones invited into the game, we were the ones who had to try to keep a straight face.

In the twentieth century, many people thinking about religion claimed that "man has finally come of age," or words to that effect, we have put off childish things and it is time we came into what is rightfully ours. (God, can you give us the keys to the world, we'd like to take it out for a spin tonight . . . ?) "Childish things" meant all religion before the present and any religion in the present that the speaker didn't like.

I'd like to suggest instead that we are not really what people thought when they said we have "come of age," and it would be better to rest content with being childlike. Child*like* is not child*ish*. The difference is that one who is childish rebels and retreats into wishful thinking, but one who is childlike presumably has some maturity, and yet is willing (as the Psalm says) not to meddle with things too hard, but rest content like a child on its mother's breast, with a quiet soul. One who is childlike does not need to pretend. One who is childlike accepts his situation. Those who are childlike can recognize that they have invented their game; those who are childish rebel in denial when their own hand in their own game is pointed out to them.

It would be easy to despair at this point, because it appears that there is no truth independent of history and culture, and more radically, that there is no truth independent of the knower. That anxiety is inevitable once you see that religions are inventions of culture, once you see that religions have a history. To sharpen the question, how can something be true if what is known depends on me, the knower? How can something really be true if it is not true for us in the same way that it is true for God? And are we not bereft, abandoned, if we cannot know, at least in part, as God knows?

That question is natural in Western culture today. It comes to everybody, whether it is spelled out or not. It assumes that the God is a being, one that might or might not exist, though we saw in chapter 5 that there are ways to understand a God who is not a being among other beings. And it assumes that the God is somewhat like us. To turn the closing question of the last paragraph on its head, Are we not bereft, abandoned, if God does not know, albeit in a larger way, as we know? The answer to the question, posed that way, is No. God does not know as we know: "my ways are not your ways, my thoughts are not your thoughts" (Isaiah 55.8). Nor are we bereft or abandoned simply because God is not like us.

Yet despair is not total, if the world is indeed real. For if the world is real, and we are real in it, then sooner or later, we have to fish or cut bait, come to some kind of appraisal of how things ultimately are. That's true even if the ultimate meaning is meaninglessness. To

## 6.1 Children's Games

say that life and the world are meaningless is still to talk about life and the world, and the act of talking about them always gives them some meaning, even if that meaning is "meaningless." But if you don't want to think of your life as ultimately meaningless, then what? Even meaninglessness would be a social construction, and any kind of positive meaning most certainly is.

What I want to suggest is that we are always in the position of children, who have imagined a world to live in. Into that world ultimate reality, what really matters in life, what really living really is, always comes, called or not, and shows itself. We can know that we have invented our own world with the materials given to us, and we can welcome ultimate reality into it, present in an analogical way as a player, but not just another player in the same way as ordinary players in the world. Why is it impossible to do this if we know this is what we are doing? We know that we do not have the perspective on our own time that later history will have, simply because we know that we *do* have a perspective on those who came before us, a perspective that is afforded only by history.

It is natural in today's somewhat strange world to think of God as an undetectable entity that interferes with the natural course of events to the advantage of those who think it exists and the disadvantage of those who do not. Such a God has consciousness and will, and its intent is like a force that acts at a distance: it can "do anything," make anything happen at will. Instead, if we start from the phrase "the way things are," the language that we have seen above in answer to the question whether it is right to embrace exposure, limitation, and need as good, blessing-bearing, things look very different. Is this really the way things are? Can this really be? How would this TWTA show itself in human life and the world? That showing-itself would be what we call "acts of God." I am told there is a French proverb that a coincidence is an event in which God wishes to remain anonymous. On that wisdom, all acts of God are anonymous. There is no "how" to acts of God, there is no kinematics nor dynamics to acts of God; the concept of God simply doesn't work that way. It is poetic, it is comical, it is ironic, and it plays on the open-ended-ness, unknowability, and unpredictability of the future. But it is not kin to physics or any other natural science. The Way Things Are shows itself in life without allowing us to jump to the conclusion that we know the mind of God or that there was the slightest interference with nature in acts of God.

How might ultimate reality show itself in ordinary everyday life? Analogically, as a player in this world-game, but not just one more player like all the others, as I said a moment ago? That we have seen already, in section 5.3, "The Far Side." If your bottom line is that life is to be embraced as good, in full view of its pains, then ultimate reality shows itself in the blessings that come with those pains (as well as with the fun parts of life; but the pains are—by definition—most of the hard work). It is always *your* view of reality, or *my* view of reality; there is no way that I can see to get out of taking responsibility for the commitment to embrace life as good. So we are always left holding the bag.

## 6.2 Creating the Beginning

Look at the history, to see the record of games invented by people, and before humans, by nature, and see how ultimate reality has entered into those games. One could find parallels enough in nature, in the natural "history" of evolution. But the full reality of invented meaning comes only with language, and so only with human life in history. The parallels in nature arise only from a very analogical reading of nature. We "read into" nature (by telling the story of nature in our language) analogs of our experience as language-capable human beings in history. It would be easy, on such a reading, to mistake evolutionary "natural history" for the model for human history. In reality, it is only the prologue, not the model. Evolution makes possible what comes later in human history. For all its wild beauty, evolution does not yet participate in the intentional processes that we know as human history.

## 6.2 Creating the Beginning

In history, human history, people were first able to remember their own actions enough to question what had gone before. Parenthetically, this requires writing; mere oral tradition, enchanting as it is, is not enough. It is actually *too* enchanting, and that is the problem. With writing, you can dispute about what happened, and you can fix details, and you can protect the details of history from turning into preposterous legends.

The move into history was a move into accepting un-natural disruption and disaster as nevertheless good-bearing. It happened only very slowly in biblical religion, over a period of centuries, maybe a millennium. In the aboriginal nature religions that humankind started with everywhere ("shamanisms"), nature is supposed to be orderly and predictable, and human life is supposed to fit into nature and be just as orderly as nature is. (This is in Eliade, 1949.) A strong nature religion has its ways to deal with chaos and disorder in nature, to restore natural order. If human society is understood as just part of nature, then human disorder can be restored to natural order. There are texts enough from the sophisticated ancient nature religions of Mesopotamia and Egypt about how to deal with human wrongdoing (Westphal, 1984). But they occur in a cultural context in which what later became nature as understood scientifically and what became human action as understood in history were not yet differentiated. And the remedies in nature religions are all natural. In the ancient world, those remedies are for the most part existential, comfort and solace without much engineering. Today, naturalistic remedies come from engineering, and for the naturalistic of mind, that is enough for all human problems. Yet we are not less grateful for triumphs of engineering even when we look also for remedies for historical problems.

The difference between chaos in nature and disorder in history is that natural disorder is not intentional. It may exemplify the random, as the weather does, but it is not deliberately intended. At least not for us, today. In the ancient world, people often attributed intention to the weather, and it took millennia to learn not to do that. One can easily find texts that do that even in the Bible, though those texts are well on the way to history. Look at Psalm 114, the earthquake Psalm that attributes geological disturbances in Israel to historical causes in the Exodus. Before it stands Psalm 29, in which God is simply Lord of the storm. That Psalm was copied from Ugaritic sources; only the name of the deity was changed. With Psalm 114 comes the entire Exodus tradition, one that is intensely focused on history. And it is not entirely clear that Psalm 114 was intended "literally" in any way that *we* would call literal. (Maybe they knew they were being ironic!)

History is different, because history and human actions really are intentional. Historical disorder (being conquered by your neighbors) can't be fixed by trying to restore the order of nature. Natural remedies don't work for historical pains. This is one reason why nature and history slowly became differentiated. Nature was feared as destructive, but history was feared as malicious or meaningless.

Writing was the root of change, even if change came slowly. For disorder becomes obvious when you can write down the events of history. At first, history was doubtless written to gratify the vanity of conquerors, and record their conquests in stone in public places so that people would see and fear. It was writing that made historical thinking possible: the ability to keep records, to create an official history, to publish an account of how things came to be the way they are. This is as true of the documents behind the Bible as it is of the archives of the Egyptian and Mesopotamian empires. But legitimation of established monarchies grows into something much bigger. Keep it in mind, for it lies in the background of what happened next.

In the texts as we have them, when Moses the shaman led the Hebrews out of Egypt he did a very un-shamanly thing, for he led them out of nature and into history, but with a difference, because here history is welcomed and embraced, not rejected as something to be fended off. To be sure, they were anxious—and said so; "were there not graves enough in Egypt, that you led us out here into the desert to die?" Were there not graves enough in nature, with the

## 6.2 Creating the Beginning

comforts of order and regularity, that you had to bring us out here into history, into disorder, first to starve and then to be eaten alive by hostile neighbors? There is a great irony in the texts—for the Hebrews left the metropolitan culture of Egypt for the desert, and in that move they also left a nature-oriented culture for life in history. You would expect to find sophisticated understanding of history in the big city and nature religion out in the wilderness. But the desert, nature in the raw, stands as a symbol for the anxieties of history, for Israel had to learn to trust in the unknown in the desert. Nature brings death, history brings meaninglessness and anxiety. The move into affirming history was partial and tentative, and biblical religion still is skittish about history. But it began here, with these texts, and it was most definitely a case of first seeing and then embracing one of the inescapable conditions of human life that had until then been rejected.

Much more than just this went on—for these people borrowed myths, borrowed legends, borrowed hymns, borrowed a world-view, and made it all their own. Borrowed is perhaps not the right word; they grew up with this world-view, and it was rightfully their own as much as anyone else's. But what they did with it was quite creative. They had inherited a suite of children's games, the world-games of the original religions of the Ancient Near East, games that everybody played just to make sense of human life. What they did with these games implies that in some ways, they realized that they were a human creation. In some dim sense, they realized that their lives were a product of history. For at the harvest festivals, when one would normally give thanks to nature for her bounty, they instead turned to history and made a conscious effort to remember the events by which they came into the Promised Land. When they came to write it all down, they put two creation stories side by side, stories that are mutually inconsistent and of quite different ages. (Sixth and tenth century BCE?) The order of events, the order in which things are created, is different; they can't both be right. They altered both stories in important ways. Readers long ago noticed that the texts in Genesis 1-2 have deleted references to nature gods that were originally part of the story. What is less often noticed are the implications of setting two inconsistent stories side by side; that pretty much means that someone knew what was going on, someone knew that these texts were a product of human history. At a minimum, the editors did, for they put the texts together, and they must have had some understanding of what they were doing. There are many cases of alternative (and often inconsistent) versions of the same story in the Pentateuch and the Former Prophets (Joshua, Judges, Samuel and Kings). The editors seem to want everybody to be heard, even when different voices told the story in different ways. This knowledge about the tension between Genesis 1 and Genesis 2 was quickly forgotten—the two stories were harmonized, and the inconsistencies were no longer noticed, and once again, the terror of history was tamed.

In biology, in the long natural history of evolution, one could find analogs aplenty of limitation embraced, though they are only analogs of what happens in human *intentional* creativity with limitation. Analogs of need might be found, simply by looking at ecological cooperation. I leave that for the reader. What is missing in natural history are analogs of exposure, for exposure requires language. Poetically, metaphorically, I can attribute intentionality to natural organisms in their struggle with limitation or common need, but I can't attribute sophisticated *language* to non-linguistic creatures. Without language, there is no way to make sense of events, no way to characterize actions. This is more elementary than you might think, for actions make sense only as parts of narratives, as parts of stories, and stories are told only in language. Cats and dogs do not tell stories, cats and dogs cannot be exposed, reproached, or called to judgement by the telling of stories. We scold pets ("Bad dog! Bad dog!"), but it is little more than operant conditioning. We can't say to the cat or the dog, "Just what did you think you were doing?" with all the implicit reproach of such a question. That requires language on the part of the dog, more language than their very limited abilities are capable of. So exposure in nature is not really possible, but exposure shows up everywhere in human history.

There are plenty of examples of exposure in the Bible, starting early. Adam and Eve are caught in the garden; Cain is caught after killing Abel; the patriarchs are embarrassed on numerous occasions, David is caught by the prophet Nathan after arranging Uriah's death and taking Uriah's wife Bathsheba. Secular history since the Bible has examples enough, were more needed. People tell stories from history, and sometimes they have to revise their stories. When new information comes to light, they are changed. Sometimes they embrace the exposure.

And so we build worlds out of words, and into those worlds comes the possibility of new life, disguised from time to time as disappointment. Sometimes it is recognized and embraced.

## 6.3 The Three Thing

Constructing a cosmos, making sense of the world and the universe, is like a game. Everything in the universe has a role to play, and there are rules of the game, rules that tell how things work, what kind of things happen and what you're supposed to do. The rules don't always tell what kind of things don't happen, except when they tell you how (not) to break the rules. Other games are usually not described; the rules for hearts don't tell you how to play bridge. Or how to play volleyball—a game that is completely different from hearts. The rules for hearts might give you a hint that bridge (or pinochle) are possible, but ball games are quite beyond the horizon of card games. And so constructing a cosmos in one civilization still leaves you surprised when you come to another civilization.

When you are "inside" the game, playing, things have a kind of order, you know what is happening. In a way, even in competitive games, you are comfortable. The world is now just the world of the game, and the world makes sense. In a funny way, playing a game is like making sense of the cosmos, as I suggested a moment ago. The "cosmos-game" has players and rules and ways to win or lose. It can even be played as a spectator sport, when the gods are the "pros" and you and I are just watching. And there are even other universes just like there are other games, in the sense that other cultures have their own ways to make sense of the universe—and other cultures can be bafflingly different from your own.

It was this way with the Indo-Europeans. For the tripartite ideology that we saw in sections 3.1 and 3.2 was a way of organizing *everything*, from the gods and regions of the cosmos to social classes, occupations in society, to tools, colors, animals, geography, foods, days and seasons, virtually everything that can be sorted or classified. At least it was that way in India (Smith, 1994), and to a lesser extent through the rest of the early Indo-European world. We return to the tripartite ideology of the Indo-Europeans, in order to look at it as part of the problem of historical relativity.

The game took somewhat different forms in the lands between Ireland and India, Norway and Greece. It was often blended with other world-views, and it was often modified as time passed. Only in India was the social organization regulated in the minute (and rigid) detail of the caste system, but there were more relaxed parallels everywhere else. The Greeks bent the symmetries of the system early, and customized it when they came among the earlier pre-Indo-European peoples who were in Greece before the invaders arrived. Something like this happened in Italy also, but a little later. Nevertheless, the basic patterns were still very much alive during the Hellenistic and Roman periods, and indeed, ample traces survive today.

The Indo-Europeans think in threes, and other language groups usually do not. At least not until after talking with Indo-Europeans. This is a "children's game" if ever there was one, and one invented when people didn't know what they were doing. It just seemed natural—"written in the stars," as they would say, and we might joke. Indeed, it was the core of world-affirming nature religion among the

## 6.3 The Three Thing

Indo-Europeans.

But is God really like this? Independently of the tripartite conceptuality of the Indo-Europeans? Let's see.

Longer ago than I can remember, a teacher offered the following as a definition of incarnation: "God comes to you in the terms of your own time." This is about a lot more than just the Incarnation of Jesus. It is about God's presence in the world, everywhere, in all activities, in history, even in nature. If God is to visit with Indo-Europeans, it is no surprise that he wears three masks, that he plays three roles simultaneously when he comes (cf. p. 22). And so when biblical religion moved into the Greek-speaking world and lost its fluency in Hebrew, it naturally thought in three-part series. This happened already in the New Testament documents, most of which were written by people who were fluent in Greek, and dubiously fluent in Hebrew or Aramaic.

How did the notion get started that God comes to you in the terms of your own time? How, indeed, did the idea get started that your own time and place might even be different from any other time or place? As nearly as I can guess, the roots of this are in the Exodus. At least it is in the Exodus that this kind of openness is both seen and affirmed as good. And affirming it as good is more than just finding it to be interesting. To say that God comes to you in the terms of your own time, you would have to suspect that other times and other places might think differently. You would have to suspect that there is something beyond nature—namely, history. Usually, the openness of history was deplored as a disruption of the order of nature, something to be feared and suppressed, not something to be affirmed as good. (We saw that in the last section.) But suppose you have noticed history, then what? You know that your neighbors' views are different from your own. (This requires the kind of routine travel that became possible only with iron technology, so for practical purposes, iron was necessary as well as writing.) You can see the social construction of reality at a gut level, because you can see that other cultures do things differently, even if you don't know about twentieth-century sociology, the *theory* of how different cultures do things differently. (We are talking about the second and first millennia BCE here.) If you still want to affirm human life in history, you pretty much have to say that God comes to you in the terms of your own time. There is no other way you could understand history.

As we have seen, the tripartite conceptual system appears in many places in the earliest Christian documents. The miracles have it—cleansings, raisings, feedings, ministering to exposure, limitation, and need. It appears in the blessings. The oldest blessing has the functions in the natural Indo-European order: "The grace of our Lord Jesus Christ, the love of God, and the fellowship of the Holy Spirit." In the end of Matthew, we see the later traditional order with the Father named before the Son. As I have said, the Indo-European order was often customized, and more customization than this would happen as the early Fathers sorted out their theology. The tripartite system appears in the teaching of Jesus, as we have already seen (p. 14): "Repent, the jig is up!; accept life in gratitude and joy; and help your neighbor in need." Here again, the three functions are encountered in exposure, limitation, and need. Perhaps Jesus knew some Greek, but there is no evidence for it if he did. If not, this three-fold organization was probably not in the teaching of Jesus originally; assuming that he spoke in Aramaic, he would not have thought in terms of the tripartite worldview. The gospel writers, who really did think and write in Greek, unconsciously imposed their own world-view on their memories of Jesus.

Does this sound farfetched? There are parallels in other cultures, when a religion moves from one language family to another. Buddhism is a very different kind of religion, but it spread in a way that is oddly similar to the spread of biblical religion. Buddhism got started in India, a very Indo-European part of the world, around the sixth century before the Common Era. And Buddhism soon moved around the mountains to China, *out* of the Indo-European world, rather than into it. But we can see some of the same kind of changes. We should expect to see

## 6.3 The Three Thing

the Indo-European ideas modified to accommodate Chinese culture. I don't think the tripartite ideology appears in Chinese Buddhism in quite the way it did in the original Indian Buddhism. But the tripartite system may not be the most conspicuous feature of Indo-European thinking that was shed. The verb to-be is peculiar in Indo-European languages, and philosophy in Indo-European cultures has an interest in "Being" that does not really appear in other places. Sure enough, when Buddhists hit the ground in China, they relax about "Being" and begin to have fun. The playfulness appears in Zen. Buddhism and biblical religion are two fairly different ways of living in the world, and each one kept its central commitments as it moved from one culture to another, but each one also made accommodations as it moved.

Is all this a project to promote the Indo-European worldview? No. Emphatically not. Even Dumézil didn't do that, as we saw in section 3.1. I am just observing how the tripartite worldview works if the world around you assumes it and you have to deal with it. There are other ways to set up radical monotheism, to set up the transformation of disappointments into blessings. What if the anthropologists should change their minds and declare all connections between a tripartite ideology and the Indo-Europeans to be a mistake, not supported by evidence? Would it change much? No, not really. The disappointments exposure, limitation, and need remain, whether or not the *series* was formed under Indo-European influences. You still have to deal with them in your life. But the series looks culturally relative, and it is best and safest to assume that it is culturally relative.

One may well ask at this point, have we relativized the Trinity? Well, yes, in a way. But it is not yet completely clear what relativizing means. The harder form of the question asks whether we are not just *projecting* the idea of the tripartite system onto reality, whether we are not just imagining it all. Does ultimate reality "really" have nothing at all to do with our cultural creation, our habit of thinking in threes? Are we just making it all up when we break things into three parts, one of which is about legitimacy and order, one of which is about action and getting things done, one of which is about nutrition and sustenance? Is this a children's game? Is this *just* a children's game? If it *is* a children's game, is that a bad thing or a good thing? Does it leave us all alone, abandoned?

Take the accusation in its harsher form, projection. Sigmund Freud's name is associated with the charge, though others before him (Feuerbach, for example) and certainly many after him think that it's all make-believe, that features of human life are being erroneously attributed to ultimate reality. I would like to suggest another meaning of projection, from geometry rather than psychology.

I have a screen-saver on my computer, a picture of a slowly rotating four-dimensional cube. (At the turn of the century it shipped with the XFree86 version of X-Windows for Linux, in xscreensaver, for those who want to see it for themselves.) Now in order to show a four-dimensional cube, you have to make some accommodations. For we can see and think in only three dimensions. And so the four-cube has to be *projected* down into three dimensions, and then projected down further into two dimensions before it can be displayed on the screen. We can know the four-cube, but only as it intersects with our three-dimensional world. This is a little like the traditional observation in Catholic philosophy that "the known is in the knower according to the mode of the knower," if that is not too big a mouthful.

This is to suggest that ultimate reality, whatever it is, is something that we know only in the conceptual terms of our own culture, our own time and place. If it is not too humiliating to admit that we do not know God as he is in himself, but only as he comes to us, this should not be a problem. We know what he tells us, and he speaks our language to us, not the language of Klingons or Romulans or the plasma wraiths of supergiant stars, or some other space-aliens. This is part of the difference between being childish and being childlike.

## 6.4 What You Mean Three, White Man?

In the 1950s on American television there was a wild West series set in Texas, starring the Lone Ranger and his faithful ally, Tonto, a native American. From time to time, they would see trouble from afar, and the Lone Ranger would declare that "we" should go and do something about it. In view of the danger of the proposed course of action, Tonto was wont to reply, "What you mean 'we,' white man?" Keep that in mind, in view of the Indo-European origins of the tripartite ideology and its place in the structure of the Trinity.

The analogy of projective geometry has more in it than we have seen. Suppose, for example, that we were to think not in Cartesian coordinates, but in spherical coordinates. In a Cartesian system, there are three coordinates, usually just called $x$, $y$, and $z$, and they are related to each other like the edges of a box. But in spherical coordinates, you think in terms of latitude, longitude, and altitude. If not altitude, then radius, the distance from the center of the earth, or the center of the coordinate system.

It is clear that you can convert from one coordinate system to the other, although the formulas are complicated. What is more, there can be more than one *Cartesian* coordinate system: all you have to do is move the box that defines the axes of the system, the axes along which you measure $x$, $y$, and $z$.

You might think at this point that, yes, other coordinate systems are possible, but they all have three coordinates; the number three can't be changed. But what is more surprising than changing from Cartesian to spherical coordinates is that you *can* change to a system with more or fewer than three coordinates. What happens, however, is that the points of space get "all scrambled up," that is, points that are neighbors in one system are not neighbors in the other system.

This feature of the analogy suggests something important about communications between radically different cultures. One culture can put "next to" each other features of life that in another culture have nothing to do with each other. I'm sure that cultural anthropologists could supply examples. George Lakoff, a linguist, found a few spectacular cases in *Women, Fire, and Dangerous Things*. But for present purposes, at least the model of projective geometry should prepare us. It may even be—and here, the analogy fails us—that in some cultures, things don't get organized always according to a fixed number of ideas. Judaism doesn't much like threes, but it does seem to be fond of groups of 1, 4, 7, 10, 13, and so on. Utes and Aztecs think in fours. Taoism doesn't set much store by arithmetic at all. Or if it does, it likes twos, paired yins and yangs.

Look at a particularly famous example from the Common Documents. It is quoted in the New Testament, but it is mistranslated there, as it was mistranslated earlier in the Greek translation of the Common Documents, the translation known as the Septuagint. Yet the mistranslation is all but inevitable, and an accurate translation is not easy. Someone asks Jesus what is the most important commandment in the Law (Mark 12.28, Matthew 22.37, Luke 10.25). It is not surprising that he answers "You shall love the Lord with all your heart, with all your soul, with all your strength." He is, of course, quoting Deuteronomy 6.5, the Shema: "Hear, O Israel, The Lord is our God, the Lord alone. you shall love the Lord your God with all your heart, with all your soul, with all your might." The Shema is the prayer that every Jew then (and still, in rabbinic Judaism) said daily. Jesus and his hearers all knew it by heart. Today, it is the lesson for Night Prayer in the Breviary for Saturdays.

What the Hebrew has in Deuteronomy is a command to love the Lord with all your *lev*, with all your *nephesh*, and with all your *me'od*. It is these three words that are hard to translate, because they are almost inevitably forced into the Indo-European tripartite conceptual system when they are translated. But they are *not* part of that three-part system of ideas. The Septuagint has *kardia*, *psuche*, and *dunamis*, which are rendered into English well enough as heart, soul, and might or strength. The Gospels squirm in their translations, as the Septuagint translators did. They try to be faithful to the original, as best they understand it. At the same time, they try to squeeze it into what they think it has to be, because everything is supposed to fit into the same three-part pattern.

But each of *lev, nephesh,* and *me'od* gets translated elsewhere in the Common Documents by words from all three of the Indo-European functions. *Lev* appears as heart, wisdom, understanding, midst, consent. *Nephesh* appears as soul, life, body, person, beast, man, mind, will, desire, self. *Me'od* appears as exceedingly, very, greatly, more, muchness.

The three words *lev, nephesh,* and *me'od,* taken in a series, constitute a progression from the inner man to all parts of his life, to the man-in-community, the human being with all his involvements in life, social, practical, economic, cultural, whatever. In other words, it is a series, but it is a series from your heart, through your person to your life in community. This is utterly different from the Indo-European way of analyzing phenomena, and it should not be forced into or even toward Indo-European categories, as it is in the Gospels, where mind, strength, and heart would appear to represent the three Indo-European functions.

Now one could complain at this point that the three-part series in the Hebrew is not a list of independent aspects of human life, but merely a progression in one aspect or dimension of life. True enough; if we are in spherical coordinates, then *lev, nephesh* and *me'od* march along the radial dimension, ignoring latitude and longitude. But in the Hebrew worldview, the differences between the three Indo-European functions don't matter and are not even enduring or stable. So why include them?

So far, we have merely noticed that when Jews think in Hebrew, they don't think in terms of the tripartite ideology. Fair enough. When Jews *do* think in Indo-European languages, the tripartite ideology shows up quickly. Philo of Alexandria (whom we saw only briefly at the beginning of section 3.1) was a first century thinker who wrote in Greek and apparently had a weak knowledge of Hebrew, at best. He was dependent on the Septuagint for the Scriptures. He has no interest in Jesus, and indeed, seems to be unaware of Jesus, but he clearly exhibits the series exposure, limitation, and need, if not exactly in those words.

The most casual search of the article "Philo" in the *Encyclopedia of Philosophy* turns up just what one would expect. A Hebrew term that is not assigned to one of the Indo-European functions in its original usage requires translation by at least three different terms in Greek, and the Greek terms are function-specific, because the Greek-speaking mind finds it difficult not to think in function-specific terms. The term is *tsedeqah*, usually just translated as righteousness. For Philo it is necessary to find three virtues in Greek to represent the original Hebrew concept; two of them appear already in the Septuagint: *dikaiosune*, justice, and *eleemosune*, mercy. Because concepts tend to be forced into one or another of the functions, justice is appropriated to right action, a second-function concept. Mercy in Philo appears as *philanthropia*, humanity, giving help to those in need of it. At this point, we have the second and third functions, lacking only the first. Philo completes the triad of virtues with *metanoia*, repentance, the missing first-function translation of the concept of *tsedeqah*. And repentance is just exactly the response to exposure which we have posited above. Interestingly also, *metanoia* was considered a vice in Greek philosophy, but a virtue for Philo and later for Christians. Philo gives us both a full tripartite analysis of the virtue of *tsedeqah* and also the peculiarly monotheistic insistence on embracing the disappointments that come in each function, because they are not barren, but bear blessings.

We saw at the start that biblical monotheism transforms the disappointments of life into blessings. Philo demonstrates this in Greek-speaking Judaism, but what would ordinary Hebrew-speaking Judaism have to say? It is the inversions of disappointment that we are interested in, and the tripartite ideology is incidental. There is a term in Hebrew, *tikkun olam*, that means approximately repair of the world,

## 6.4 What You Mean Three, White Man?

and this idea is probably the general counterpart of what I am calling transformation of disappointments. Whatever may be said of *tikkun olam*, it may confidently be said that *shuv*, the word for repentance in Hebrew, is *not* function-specific in the way that *metanoia* is in Philo's Greek. Joseph Soloveitchik's *Halakhic Man* has a great deal to say about *shuv*, repentance, and it really doesn't fit into a tripartite series.

What happens when Christianity moves out of the Indo-European world and into Asia (as Buddhism did, many centuries earlier)? Take for example the Korean experience of Christian theology. I have in mind Jung Young Lee's book, *The Trinity in Asian Perspective*. In Korea, the Trinity appears as an instance of the Confucian anthropology of the family: father, mother, son, instead of the three functions from the Indo-European world. The symbols of yin and yang appear, and heaven appears as father, earth as mother, and humans as children. Earth is feminine, and is sometimes assimilated to the Holy Spirit, also feminine. There is a detailed connection with the I Ching and the eight basic trigrams. There is also a serious historical connection with Confucian thought. I am assuming that the radically monotheistic transformation of the pains of life into blessings appears here, as it has earlier in biblical religion. It certainly has taken on a new garb, a new cultural idiom.

What about the *Tao Te Ching*, another mindspring of East Asian religion? It is completely innocent of the Indo-European tripartite ideology. And it doesn't have much in common with biblical religion — at first glance. According to legend, the *Tao Te Ching* was written by Lao Tzu, a Chinese sage in the sixth century BCE. It is a collection of eighty short poems, with a verse style somewhat like the wisdom books of the Common Documents: Proverbs, or Sirach. It is full of paradoxes and twists of logic that the mind can play with for hours — or years — on end.

Lao Tzu has no interest in history. He doesn't have the candid up front in-your-face inversion of the pains of life, but he does have something hauntingly like it, and it gets repeated many times, in many forms. Someplace, a translator of the *Tao Te Ching* remarked that he found more than seventy pairs of opposed concepts, of which the duo *yin* and *yang* is only the prototype. Usually, Lao Tzu likes one better than the other, but rarely, if ever, will he categorically bless one and condemn the other. There are always circumstances when his favorite is not the way to go. At the heart of yin, one will find yang; at the heart of yang, one will find yin. Is this the transformation of pains into blessings? Not obviously; but I wouldn't rule it out. It sure sounds like the raw material for that transformation. I have seen rumors of a translation of the Gospel of John into Chinese that begins, "In the beginning was the Tao, and the Tao was with God, and the Tao was God . . . ." What was happening? Other people have seen the romance that Taoism can hold for biblical religion.

What about other, non-Indo-European cultures? I know rumors of only two, and even minimal details of only one. In the American southwest and Mexico, the Utes and Aztecs and their kin had a characteristically four-part view of the world, modeled on the points of the compass, north, south, east, and west. Such four-part series do appear in other cultures, but in the Uto-Aztecan world, they are the central and organizing system. Animals, plants, colors, seasons, foods, weather, gods, regions, and people are all arranged around the points of the compass. Most of the Aztec literature was destroyed by the Conquistadors, and so what is left is fragmentary and tantalizing. There is no sense of transcendence of the divine that seems essential in biblical religion; everything is part of nature, whether visible or invisible. And so it would be hard to find Aztecan counterparts for the transcendence of the deity in Greek philosophy or in the Bible. But surely, one could ask, "What are the characteristic pains at each of the four compass points, and what would it mean for each of those pains to be transformed into a blessing? I don't know how to do that, and maybe nobody *has* done it, but surely it could have been done in 1500, even if it can't be done now. Unlike aboriginal cosmologies of Central America, Bantu cultures are still very much alive. The Bantu family of languages and cultures in Africa is only beginning to be studied. More effort would doubtless yield rich rewards.

So what have we seen, how far have we come? We have seen that biblical religion is about affirming all of life as good, hard parts included. And we have seen that to do that, you have to speak the language of the culture you live in. (And what other language could you speak?!) In the space that remains in this chapter and the next, I would like to return to the more important of the two ideas: the transformation of pains into blessings.

## 6.5 History, Relativity, and Pluralism

The consciousness that our religion, our worldview, our science, our ethics, and our cosmology are all social products, that they are different in different cultures and different centuries, has hit home in the twentieth century in a way that is radical compared to any previous time in Western or biblical culture. We worry about it, we are perplexed by it, we wonder whether there are any binding standards of right and wrong anymore. (Actually, we usually speak of absolute standards of right and wrong, and the choice of the word *absolute* says that we have not entirely escaped from non-historical or anti-historical ways of thinking that we inherit from the Enlightenment.) Biblical religion knew about its own choices, and it knew that its choices *were* choices and not written in the stars, because it spoke in so many words about choices. The great Deuteronomic sermon at the end of Joshua puts the question to the assembled multitude of Israel: which gods will you worship? They knew it was a choice. But they didn't know it like we know it, because we have a bigger menu of choices than they had. Oddly, we often hide our choices and pretend necessity instead.

In many ways, we have become a very naturalistic culture once again, even though the common religion, variants of Christianity and Judaism, is supposedly a historical religion. Only Evangelicals, Fundamentalists, and people who live in a lectionary know much about the

Bible. In *Waters* I've already challenged Fundamentalist biblical interpretation, and so here I merely note my respect for Fundamentalists and Evangelicals, and also my disagreements, without spelling them out. We take our understanding of the world from the modern scientific understanding of nature. We trust the sciences, and we admire the sciences, for good reason. Yet unlike pre-modern naturalisms, we know that science is progressive, we know that we have some control over its applications in engineering. Above all, we know that scientific theories are not permanent, even though much of what they discover really is permanent. We trust that when scientific theories are overthrown, it is progress and not a catastrophe. Indeed, the revisability of scientific knowledge is one reason we place so much trust in it. One could say accordingly that historical faith shines brightest in the modern world in the sciences. The sciences make progress at the cost of limiting their inquiry to nature, but they have earned the trust we place in them because they think about scientific progress historically, because they are always open to revision and correction. Yet in religion, we still seek "absolute" (i.e., ahistorical) truth. The irony is that, whether we know it or not, in the study of nature, we think historically, but in a supposedly historical religion, we seek to escape from history. We know when we think historically that not all things are derivable from nature, contrary to what a truly naturalistic culture would say. Even if we can deal historically with the sciences, how to deal historically with history itself continues to frustrate us. We can think historically, with subtlety and nuance about human actions, but we are extremely reluctant to spell out what we are doing when we think historically. The best we ever do is cynical wisecracks about "spin" in political narratives.

Why modern science was accompanied by a more comprehensive naturalism is unclear, but that seems to be what happened. The story is told by Alexandre Koyré and E. A. Burtt. The centuries before the new science had a much richer view of human life, human action, and God. C. S. Lewis's *The Discarded Image* tells a little of that richness.

## 6.5 History, Relativity, and Pluralism

In any case, our culture has by stages extended the scientific view of things to all of life, not just nature itself. Whether we knew it or not, in the same move, we tried to use nature as a way to get out of the anxieties of living in history.

Many things changed in the seventeenth and eighteenth centuries, and only one was a reconception of action as a kind of physical causation. What showed up, slowly, over 200 years, was that human action really is *not* just a kind of physical causation. History emerged in clarity after it was first misunderstood in terms of physics. Historical *method* emerged in clarity after people assumed that the received accounts of the past were literally true. The literal meanings didn't work. Out of that failure came modern biblical criticism and the critical study of secular history as well, in the nineteenth century. Religion (meaning Christianity) was in trouble, and some people thought that they could rescue it (and replace the traditional explanations) by showing that it was the evolutionary culmination of the history of religions. By the end of the century, this, too, wasn't working. What was left was radical relativity of religion to history and culture, and a pluralism of world religions.

History, relativity, and pluralism are the challenge to biblical religion today, even more so than science. People who *think* science is the main challenge to biblical religion do so because they still tacitly think that biblical religion is about an undetectable entity that interferes with the natural course of events to the advantage of those who think it exists and the disadvantage of those who do not. That mistake is fairly easy to get out of. But the next question is, *then* what do you do? For it is not just divine action as a species of physical causation that is in trouble—we might also have to give up claims of absolute truth in religion. When God interfering with nature is gone, history, relativity, and pluralism stand out conspicuously as challenges today. I would like to claim that history is a species of exposure, relativity is a species of limitation, and pluralism is a species of need. Historical scholarship shows that the received traditional accounts in the Bible are not all true.

(Nor are they all fictional, by the way.) Relativity means that religion, even biblical religion, is not only a human invention but is different in every age and culture. Religious pluralism means that people who have no particular interest in Jesus still have a claim on us, simply as our neighbors.

Critical history is embarrassing: it has shown that the history of biblical religion was not always as the literalists, traditionalists, and casual readers thought it was. Sometimes it has shown that biblical religion was not very attractive. Exposure shows both sin and finitude, and both are embarrassing. Critical scholarship excels at making Christian history embarrassing. Yet even if critical scholars tell us that the story is not one of a pristine deposit of perfect religion guaranteed from on high, they also tell us that it is a story of the slow, gradual emergence of world-affirming historical religion from world-affirming nature religion, with not-infrequent relapses backwards. It is not a history of despair, but for those open to it, one of hope.

A small digression into the method of critical history may help before we come to relativity and pluralism. That method was described by Ernst Troeltsch ("Ernst Who?," in *Waters*) as one of criticism, correlation, and analogy. By criticism he meant that the historian is responsible for his judgements about the past, and those judgements are always open to future criticism and revision. They are not absolute. By correlation he meant that causal explanation in history has to be in terms of other historical events, not interference from outside history. That rules out interference from the deity, in particular. And by analogy, he meant that we can't claim things happened in the past for which we have no experience, not even by analogy, in the present. That rules out "miracles" as exceptions to natural laws. Yet each one of these losses turns out to bear a gain beyond price: When absoluteness is surrendered, we get the openness to correction that we know and honor in the natural sciences. Actually, it was in biblical religion before it was in the sciences, for those who know the Bible. Modern science grew up in a predominantly Christian culture, and internalized its Christian

## 6.5 History, Relativity, and Pluralism

values to the core. But, however ironic it may be, today we know openness to correction in the sciences better than we do in religion. When divine action by interference in this world is surrendered, we get a real history that challenges us far more radically than any dubious claims of interference could. If divine action is conceived not as interference but as ultimate reality showing itself in this world, we are better off. And when "miracles" are surrendered, what results is a gospel that actually offers us something in real life, life as we know it here and now. Thus come the benefits of critical history.

When cultural relativity is added to critical history, it's clear that we can no longer claim that other people invented their own religions, but God invented ours. We invented ours, just like any other religion. That can leave us feeling alone and abandoned. We saw as much in the previous sections in this chapter. But absoluteness is not given to creatures, and relativity is part of creaturehood. Trying to get out of relativity is trying to get out of creaturehood. And relativity does not mean nihilism, it just means that relative to your own time and culture, you really do know what's right and what's wrong.

Religious pluralism confronts us in the form of other religions that are not very impressed with the claims about Jesus and the Bible. Yet we all share a common world, and we need each other. The record of pluralism in the Bible, as Edward Hobbs recovered it (1973), tells a tale of many different tribes and nature-religions coming together in a unity that could only be historical, not just natural. If it happened then, why can't it happen again today? I don't know how it could happen again today, but I think it should. We have heard enough of the "convert or be damned" posture of the missionaries of the nineteenth century. Other cultures than the West can think historically, and they can find blessing in history. That means they can do world-affirming historical religion, religion of the biblical type. For them, the place to start is always by recovering their own history. The immediate task is simply more of what is happening already—getting to know other religions and other cultures. In the West, we don't know enough of the sacred texts of other religions. That task alone will take decades, at a minimum; it may take centuries.

The problems of history, relativity, and pluralism are unsolved, but I record them for the reader because they are the central task for biblical religion today. In effect, the challenge for those who are most "Pro-Life," the conservatives, takes the form of asking whether they (you, we) are pro-life enough to embrace the pains of cultural disruption when those pains come as history, relativity, and pluralism, species of exposure, limitation, and need. The challenge for the "enlightened" is not to abandon world-affirming historical religion or history itself when they are shown not to fit traditional accounts or Enlightenment canons of reason.

# Chapter 7

# In The End

## 7.1 Against Theodicy

The focus of this book sometimes gets called the problem of evil. One of the modern solutions goes by the technical name of *theodicy*. Even if the solution offered here is not a theodicy, readers will inevitably know the possibility of doing a theodicy, and it is worth some careful distinctions to make clear what is and what is not being proposed here. The word *theodicy* appears with Gottfried Wilhelm Leibniz, in the eighteenth century, and it means "justification of God." Leibniz was a diplomat, intellectual socialite, librarian, physicist, mathematician, and philosopher. He published a book called *Theodicy* in 1710. It is a defense of God against charges of malice, ignorance, and incompetence. The problem gets set up by asking why, if God is all-knowing, all-powerful, and truly benevolent, there is still evil in the world. The solutions offered by theodicy in defense of God appear to be very rational and reasonable, but in the end, I think, they are vicious. Unraveling them will require looking at the presuppositions of theodicy, whether in Leibniz's version or any other.

Very few people in this world are wrong about everything, and theodicists are not an exception. They are quite right when they point out the unreasonableness of those who want natural laws occasionally suspended for their own benefit, and the unreasonableness of those who want their own human moral freedom suspended when they don't like what they themselves have done with their own freedom. As much goes for those who think they can have other people's freedom suspended without suspending their own at the same time. So far, the theodicists are right. But these cautions, sensible as they are, do not really touch the anguish and affliction that gets called the problem of "evil." The horror of the destruction of human life is more than this common sense can deal with. Theodicy would like to have a God who is rational as humans understand rationality, who is good as humans understand goodness and benevolence, whose acts follow a rather simple human model of action, and who accounts rationally for the pains of human life. Above all, theodicy wants explanations, rational explanations. Often the quest for rational explanations is undertaken to satisfy people, both outsiders and insiders, who want rational explanations. Their questioning makes it look like rational explanations are possible and even available.

As reasonable as that sounds, I think the central claims and goals of theodicy work out in a way that is morally very ugly. For it tries to rationalize evil, and ends up by effectively justifying evil. The problems are more than a little complicated, but let's see if at least some of them can be untangled.

The term *theodicy* original means the rational justification of God in face of charges of evil against him. This is one way in theology, but not the only way, of meeting the pains of life. It is not the program of this book. Sociology borrows the term "theodicy" from theology, and there, it means more sociodicy than theodicy, the justification of society to its members. Societies, unlike God, really do have to answer to human questioners. I am indebted to Ethan Moore for the term "sociodicy." A good background source for more details is Peter Berger's *Sacred Canopy* (1967, chapter 3, "The Problem of Theodicy."). Whatever may happen in sociology, our problem is in

## 7.1 Against Theodicy

theology. The hazards of theodicy for theology are explored in D. Z. Phillips's *Belief, Change and Forms of Life* (1986).

The line of argument in theodicy, whether or not you believe the conclusion, starts by assuming that God is omniscient, omnipotent, and benevolent, and despite any denials, it gives very human meaning to omniscience, omnipotence, and benevolence. That is, God can do anything, he can make anything happen, he knows everything, and he wants only our good. Yet evil exists. Or so the argument begins. It continues in various ways with different people, and supposedly God gets defended and acquited; at least acquited of being malicious. Sometimes people say he is less than omniscient, sometimes less than omnipotent in order to secure that acquittal. Some are convinced. Many remain unconvinced.

If the problem is to be unraveled, several threads need to be pulled. The first, and easiest, is that people silently assume that God is just like us, except "more so," or "better." God has been turned into a human being writ large, and we have forgotten that it is we who have anthropomorphized God, in an analogy that we ourselves created ("Children's Games," above).

Another assumption is that the god of theodicy can simply make things happen however he pleases, and this is the assumption that causes the most offense. It is usually the only one that ever gets spelled out. For if the evils of this life are consciously intended by a being that knows as we know (except more) and can make things happen—as we do when we write fiction, say—then I think the problem is unsolvable. *That* god is guilty as charged. That god is the god of theodicy (and of analytic philosophy of religion). Incidentally, if a human had the kind of knowledge and power ascribed to that god, he would qualify as a narcissistic brat, though debatably a nice narcissistic brat. So far as I can see, that god does not exist, and its non-existence does not make it holy—unlike the God of the Bible, the God of radical monotheism, the God of world-affirming historical religion.

Anthropomorphic ideas about God creep in surreptitiously, for people tend to forget that in analogies in theology, there are usually more things different than there are alike between ultimate reality and the human experience we employ to explain it. The caution against this move is stated very early, in Isaiah 55.8: "My thoughts are not your thoughts, my ways are not your ways." One might add that God's *power* is not like human power, neither human power in real life nor human power in writing fiction.

Another tacit assumption easily sneaks in with these, one made in the activity of philosophical inquiry, not in any of its stated premises: that rational explanations of the pains of life are possible. Above all, theodicy seeks rational explanations. Second only to that goal is the quest for logical proof, and with it security against those who would disagree. Unlike philosophers, who rush in where even fools fear to tread, believers occasionally take Isaiah's caveat to heart, and so the worst damage of theodicy sometimes gets averted. If Isaiah's warning is not enough, D. Z. Phillips takes a similar position (1986).

The deepest and trickiest assumption in the "problem of evil" is that the pains of life are evil. Pain and wrongdoing can be lumped together for the moment, for here we complain against both alike, because they both hurt. We complain, but there is no easy answer to the pains of life. We have to ask why, but that doesn't mean we have to concoct answers. What happens next is not obvious. For to whom do we complain? Almighty Nothing? Almighty Nothing doesn't answer, at least not simply or obviously. If we transform Almighty Nothing into a humanoid God, then we court the risks of theodicy—rationalizing the pains of life when they are not rational. If we then blame God, and turn away, a choice has been made. It is a confessional choice, not one that could be derived from something more basic. It presupposes that there *should* be meaning in the pains of life, and then responds in blame when there is not. It is not the only possible choice, and not the choice explored in this book. If instead, we remember that Almighty Nothing is not exactly like a human being, we can do other things than just turn away in blame. We still cry out to God, even to

## 7.1 Against Theodicy

Almighty Nothing, and say, "why did you do this to us?" Examples abound in the Psalms of adversity. What do we do when Almighty Nothing doesn't gives us answers as we would like? We just bear the pains, meaninglessness included. And in that, surprisingly, we are not alone, and not without God, for we see God coming into this world to be with us in this good world, bearing—and enjoying—all of it with us, including its pains, even its meaningless pains. Meaninglessness is not to be given meaning, it can only be borne. It can be borne in trust and hope or in despair and defiance. Trust and hope are the way of radical monotheism. And defiance can grow into hope and trust.

Faith trusts that meaning (*logos*, in Christianity) comes into the world and takes upon itself meaninglessness. That's very traditional, and it appears again in *Salvifici Doloris*. To walk in the way of the Cross is to participate in that suffering, to take upon oneself meaninglessness voluntarily, or, more precisely, to consent when involuntary meaninglessness comes unavoidably, rather than rebel against it in defiance. Readers of *Fear and Trembling* hear this in Kierkegaard. Often we *start* in rebellion, but what starts in rebellion changes in the work of grieving and becomes faith, trust, hope, and even creativity. We are converted by stages—that is part of the way of the pilgrim, part of being one "on the way," *in statu viatoris*, in the traditional Latin. As the conversion works on us, we do not do everything ourselves, for the change in us comes as a gift of grace, even when we don't see it, feel it, or know it.

To say that meaning comes into the world and takes upon itself meaninglessness is the very opposite of theodicy. For theodicy is the desperate attempt to demonstrate meaning in human suffering (and thereby incidentally to justify it). To say that meaning comes into the world and takes upon itself the burden of meaninglessness is a confessional commitment, but theodicy wants something else, a deduction, a proof, something it can use against those who don't believe, against those who don't share this confessional commitment. But there is no rejoinder, no refutation, no rebuttal, no answer to those who don't share this confessional commitment. That's in the nature of a confessional commitment.

Jean-Paul Sartre apparently defined bad faith as making choice look like necessity (Berger 1967, pp. 93–94). Bad faith enables you to evade responsibility. Religion can foster bad faith, and the latter is a very effective bulwark against meaninglessness. Bad faith can be a source of inner strength, enabling you to meet any meaninglessness with confidence. Something like that is happening in theodicy, for it makes the choice to consent to suffering look rational and explicable when it is not. The choice is legitimate, but that does not make it necessary, nor does it make the pains of life rational or explicable. Religion can also expose bad faith as less than candid and foster good faith, the honesty that acknowledges confessional commitments and willingly bears the acute anxiety that goes with them. Bad faith gets one out of that anxiety.

## 7.2 Sauce For the Goose

Often for theodicy, the problem is someone else's suffering, and then bad faith becomes ugly. People who really suffer usually don't do theodicy. They know they don't know the meaning of their suffering. People who do theodicy on behalf of other people's suffering are generally trying to get out of helping those other people.

Trouble begins when the pains of life are called evil, for then, you have turned the pains of life into something that you can take offense at, or to be fussy, you turn them into an excuse to take offense at the world, or God, or *life*. In other words, the part of the problem that says there is evil in the world has quietly written off as barren the pains of life, written off as no-good the pains of life. When it is someone else's pain, this is very convenient. Then you don't have to sit with the other person in need, you don't have to acknowledge a common humanity with the other person in pain. And that means you don't really have to look for the good in your own pains, either. Sauce for the goose is

## 7.2 Sauce For the Goose

sauce for the gander.

Look at it all from another side. What *do* you do when you meet someone else in need? Someone else in trouble? Someone else in affliction? For the problem of evil contains some bizarre twists in its logic. It is easy to say that the pains of life bear blessing when the pains are not your own. Then you can dismiss other people's pains as good for them.

The test comes in a remarkably simple way. When you say that the pains of life, someone else's pains, bring a blessing, bring good, are you willing to share in that good? And share in the pains that brought it? Are you willing to be consistent? Are you willing to acknowledge a common humanity with those who suffer? Even crooks, cripples, psychos and bag ladies?

When other people's pains are relatively small, you can sometimes say to them,

> This is your life, incidentally with some pains in it; do
> you want it or not?

Are you going to accept it with gratitude, or resentment? Joy or whining? Do something with it, or refuse it? Pass it on to other people, or will it die with you? But when the pains are large, and when they are distributed unfairly, you really cannot tell the other person how to live. You cannot live other people's lives for them, and they are entitled to be respected in their own choices. The question can be horrific. It is never trivial.

More generally, and even when the other person's pains are large, suffering mounting to affliction, what can be said? Not any kind of instructions, directives, commands, accusations, patronizing encouragement, or moralizing. But an offer can be made, something like this:

> We affirm your goodness and the goodness and worth
> of your life, whether or not you do. We will support
> you in that goodness, although that is not a blank check.

We won't support you in attempts to deny your own goodness.

That is an offer and not a command, not preaching. If it is backed up with real support, it is not condescending, nor is it pity. It can be com-passion, that is, co-suffering. To be sure, language is usually ambiguous, and what is meant one way can be misunderstood in another. But at least this much is possible.

Consider in detail only the example of disability, for it provides a window into American culture today. A newly disabled person learns real fast that the able-bodied can't bear the pain of his or her disability. She has to bring them through it, she has to carry them at a time when she would rather they carried her. The disabled learn how to put the able-bodied at ease quickly. Usually this is done with body language, because there is not time to instruct strangers in long windy explanations. (Strangers don't listen, anyway, because they are too busy "helping," and they always think they know better than the disabled what needs to be done.) For the record, when I meet a disabled person, I don't know, and cannot know, what the other person's disability is like "from the inside," *and I don't have to know*. It is not necessary to feel guilty for not doing something that is impossible.

The problem is pity, and the disabled have to bring the stranger past pity if anything like a normal human relationship is to be possible. Sometimes the disabled person runs into a so-called able-bodied person whose pity is invincible and incorrigible. For the AB to give up pity would be too costly—too costly in terms of the AB's own *self*-image. The AB would have to think of *himself* in a completely different way if he gave up thinking of the disabled as pathetic. He would have to think of himself as a person just like the disabled, and think of the disabled as people just like himself. How embarrassing!

Leviticus 19.18 is usually translated "you shall love your neighbor as yourself," but it would make better sense as "you shall love your neighbor as *one like* yourself." Love of neighbor is clear enough; love of self is more like just self-maintenance. But to think of the neighbor as like me? Or even worse, to think of myself as like the grubby grabby tacky neighbor?

The first task is not just to offer help. (Usually help is not needed at all.) Before help comes respect for the other person, but not even that is really the first task. The first task is to revise your own self-image, so that you can see yourself as one just like the other person. Think of yourself as a crook, a cripple, a schizo, or a bag lady. Without that change of mind, without that change of image, helping the other is just a way to stay in control, and so to fend off the deeper claim of the needy. Once they have been "helped," you no longer need think of yourself as just folks like them. Such help is pity, and pity is a form of contempt.

Why is it so hard to see oneself as just like the disabled? Because to do that would be to embrace limitation as something bearing blessing. Never mind exposure; getting out of limitation and need is what this culture is about (see section 7.4). Yet the disabled are capable of embracing life as good in full view of its limitations; we do it every day. Those who see themselves as able-bodied seem to have difficulty with this.

## 7.3 You Are Not Alone

How do you make it work? Indeed, *can* a basic life orientation like this work?

Perhaps the best thing to say is, "You are not alone." One does not do this alone, one does not embrace exposure, limitation, and need alone, one does not find blessing in the pains of life alone. If you should choose to embrace life, simply *life*, as good, you are not alone. There are other people with you when life hurts. Things can seem lonely enough; there are times when you are alone and abandoned. Such times are terrifying to imagine, and appalling to look back on in life or in history. People certainly have faced disaster and affliction alone in faith.

Were they really alone? Yes and no. In the simple sense, yes, and that simple sense should not be denied. But when people grow up in the faith, they grow up in community, in the company of others. We learn to trust from other people, confident in the blessings in life, whatever may come. More than one person has answered, when asked why he became a Christian, "because I want what they have." It is the same for Jews, and it is always that way. Always. The Great Bag Lady of History is a community, not just a collection of individuals.

There is a story on the internet told to illustrate saving acts of God. Someplace in the upper Mississippi valley, it rained, and it began to flood, as sometimes happens in those parts in the Spring. Here is the form in which the story came to me:

There was a man called him Jim, who lived near a river. Jim was a very religious man. It began to rain, and floods were forecast. A neighbor came to offer a ride in his pickup. Jim declined, confident that God would take care of him. A day later, the river rose over the banks and flooded the town, and Jim was forced to climb onto his porch roof. While sitting there, a man in a boat came along and told Jim to get in the boat with him. Jim said "No, that's OK. God will take care of me." So, the man in the boat drove off.

The water rose, so Jim climbed onto his roof. Then another boat came along and the person in that one told Jim to get in. Jim replied, "No, that's OK. God will take care of me." The person in the boat then leaves.

The water rises even more, and Jim climbs on his chimney. Then a helicopter comes and lowers a ladder. The woman in the helicopter tells Jim to climb up the ladder and get in. Jim tells her "That's OK." The woman says "Are you sure?" Jim says, "Yeah, I'm sure God will take care of me.

Finally, the water rises too high and Jim drowns. Jim gets up to Heaven and is face-to-face with God. Jim says to God "You told me you would take care of me! What happened?" God replied, "Well, I sent you a pickup truck, two boats and a helicopter. What else did you

## 7.3 You Are Not Alone

want?"

We laugh, of course. What the joke says about divine action is that we shouldn't ask to see God's ID before getting into the neighbor's pickup truck. All you can *see* is your neighbor, and his license is expired. He didn't renew it because he had too many parking tickets. Don't even wait for the boats or the helicopter. Just get in.

Yet we want proof, assurance that it is God who comes to save us. In the afterlife, we want the beatific vision, to see God himself. (The alternative tradition is the Heavenly Banquet, which is not quite the same thing.) We don't want God to be Almighty Nothing, we want God to be *something*, preferably something we can reliably know as "existing." Yet the Lord of History and Master of Irony is none other than Almighty Nothing himself.

We bring our problems to God, our joys and our sorrows. We ask Why?, and nothing answers. We listen to God, and when we do, Almighty Nothing gently returns us to this world, to our neighbors. It covers us with its hand when it passes by, so that we cannot see it directly. It comes to us in our neighbors, even in our enemies. Edward Beutner once said, of the Good Samaritan: "I'm at the mercy of my enemy, and none the worse for it."

In our joys and pains, in anguish and thanksgiving, we reach for transcendence. We start out with a protest, in exasperation, with "How can I respond in covenantal trust?" Then we complain in anguish, meaning "I am devastated," and then we complain, crying for help. We start by asking "How could I trust?" in the rhetorical sense that presupposes that I cannot, and then slowly, we ask "How can I trust?" in the open sense that seeks a positive answer. Thus does transcendence gently turn our quest for what we cannot know back to what we can know and what we can do about it. Transcendence is safeguarded. And we have neighbors.

Our neighbors bring us comfort, in many senses of that familiar word. Comfort can mean solace, emotional support, togetherness, and it can mean practical help. Comfort can also mean strength. It is the ability to deal with the hard parts of life. In effect, our faith is shared, and that means that from time to time, other people do my believing for me. Not only is faith a shared enterprise, but other people sustain me in my times of unbelief. I depend on them, and they depend on me. If you can stand some heavy-duty language, it is a distributed ontology of faith. Like distributed computing: the job gets done, but not all on one computer. Faith is real, but if we miss its distributed character, we misunderstand it badly. Basic life orientation is shared in common.

Return to the terror of abandonment, betrayal, affliction. When people of faith are left alone, are they really alone? Yes and no. In the here and now, they are abandoned. In the sense of being emdbodied in a community of faith, no. Their fellows are present to them in faith. And so there is a certain irony in saying that they (we) are not alone. If the irony is forgotten, it would be better just to say that the afflicted are alone. That, at least, is a challenge to bystanders: are you going to leave them alone? But if there are bystanders to be challenged, then in some larger sense, none of us are alone. And we are back to the irony.

There is a story in Luke very much like the story about the man in the flood who insisted that God, not his neighbor, come to save him. Two believers are walking along, feeling very alone and abandoned. They are near despair, because the promises of God that they expected to see fulfilled have ended in disaster. A stranger joins them, and apparently the stranger has done his homework, because the stranger walks them through the texts (we would suspect he has the four great Servant Songs in Deutero-Isaiah in mind), and he shows them that the promises were not broken. They sit down to eat, and begin in prayer. The text is delicate: "And their eyes were opened and they recognized him; but he had vanished from their sight." The stranger, of course, is labeled as Jesus. But why, please tell me why, why am I supposed to take this text literally? As far as I can see, it has all the hallmarks of irony, just like the story from the internet about the man in a flood: in the stranger Jesus' friends experienced Jesus again. We would do it easily with special effects in the movies today. That is the challenge of the Emmaus story: can you accept God coming to you incognito in real life? If the story is taken figuratively, it promises good and blessing in everyday life today. If the story is taken literally, it validates the despair of those who think they really are abandoned, who think that death is really the seal of disaster and meaninglessness in life, who think that the only hope is to escape from death via immortality.

## 7.4 Clearings

Perhaps the claim of this book can be summarized in the issue that tells where life hurts in America today. Abortion is a clearing, a place where you can see what people are doing with their lives. The ending of life is a clearing, and there people want euthanasia, to get out of the unpleasant parts of dying. It may seem a digression and a sectarian imposition on the reader to look at how this book gets applied in real life. I don't think so. There are three reasons for this section. The first is candor with the reader about what the implications really are. The second comes from being disabled and watching euthanasia creep up on the disabled in American society today: it is a duty to speak out. Silence is immoral. The third comes from a need for balance. My disagreements with "traditional" conservatives are plain on every page; that I have even deeper disagreements with Liberal Theology as it is practiced today should also be indicated. I would like to disabuse the conceit of those Liberals who think, in their sophistication, that they can have biblical religion without the pains that come with it. In competing claims to represent authentic Christianity, the "conservatives" are confused, but less than fully pro-life Liberals have more serious problems.

Abortion and euthanasia are only a clearing, not the starting point for faith and ethics. This clearing shall pass, one way or another, and be replaced by others in due time. But for the present, at the end of the twentieth century and the beginning of the twenty-first, these quarrels show what people are doing with their lives, they show the larger shape of their lives. That's why they are called life issues.

In plain English, these are utilitarian homicides: homicides on grounds of "quality of life." Someone's quality of life will suffer unacceptably if we allow this person to be born alive, or to live any longer. That's what utilitarianism is: maximizing pleasure and minimizing pain, often not the pleasure or pain of the one to be killed but of the family and bystanders. Utilitarians are quite candid about this: they want to maximize not the happiness of any particular individual, but the sum total of happiness integrated over everybody. That means that if they can make most people a lot happier by eliminating a few, utilitarianism licenses just such eliminations.

I do not know how the debate about abortion in civil law will turn out. At stake is the character of American society. A society that tolerates the utilitarian homicides is barbaric, even though its barbarism be cloaked in wealth beyond the dreams of avarice of any earlier civilization. Opposition to the utilitarian homicides in civil law is based on opposition to that barbarism, on a respect for life that is necessary to undergird basic liberties and any semblance of humane civilization. As with race discrimination, the leaders of the fight for justice have been some of the churches. But the logic of the campaign against legal race discrimination was not simply religious. We expect you not to engage in race discrimination, regardless of your religious commitments. Likewise, we expect you not to indulge in utilitarian homicides, regardless of your religious commitments.

Whatever happens in civil law, one thing seems clear. As important as the lives of the unborn (and the hurt women) are, they are not the only issue that appears in abortion. Mostly we tend to think of abortion as just an ethical issue. It is that; indeed, it is the gut social issue of our time. Abortion is also more than that, it is a window into a broader and more radical question of faith, of what people are committed to in the end. The slogan "pro-life" names the issue: are you pro-*life*, even when life is hard or difficult or inconvenient or painful? This question appears all the time, for women *and* men, not just when a woman has

## 7.4 Clearings

to make decisions about children.

Are you pro-life? When life hurts? Are you pro-life when life catches you red-handed, leaves you exposed, and people can see you for who you really are, not the person you would like to appear to be? Are you pro-life when life has you up against the wall, when its limitations leave you without the choices you would like? Are you pro-life when life comes to you as someone else who needs your help? When you had other plans?

Exposure, limitation, and need. These are incidentally the reasons why most abortions are performed: The unborn child, if allowed to be born alive, would spell out what the parents have been doing, make it impossible for people to ignore it. Or it would impose limitations on the parents that they would rather not bear, and it would bring its needs to them when they had other plans. About the medically unattractive, the disabled, the dying who are dying too slowly: The desire for euthanasia comes precisely because some folks want to stiff-arm the needs of these people.

Exposure, limitation, and need. The disappointments of life. What does your heart cling to and rely upon? Avoiding them? Avoiding them in favor of some definition of happiness? In favor of the devices and desires of your own heart? Or do you embrace *all* of life, pains included, as good, as created by God, as bearing blessing, even when that blessing cannot be seen in the here and now?

The Supreme Court, in Planned Parenthood v. Casey (1992), said that a generation of Americans had structured their lives in reliance on the availability of abortion and contraceptives. They put their finger on the real issue: the utilitarian homicides are a clearing in which you can indeed see what people are doing with their lives. Some need access to the utilitarian homicides, some do not. Whether you need access to the utilitarian homicides depends on how you live, how you structure your life, your relationships to others, your commitments, your family, your job, your plans. These homicides grew out of contraceptives, a technology that works to breed a pervasive disrespect. That's not how it was marketed, of course.

The consequences for culture and society? In the old days, people used to court and then marry. Nowadays, they play house. When four-year-olds play house, it is enchanting and beautiful. When twenty-four-year olds play house, it is destructive to everybody. Anybody can see this who has eyes in his or her head, for we all know people who have been hurt. For the obtuse, for those in denial, survey research has amply confirmed the damage (Eberstadt, 2004). We pray in heartfelt anguish for the success of the people who court this way, even though we know the statistics and the reality. The devastation wreaked on society by the marriages that later fail is well chronicled and widely lamented. But lament is about as far as the response gets: for we can't live without "reproductive technologies," can we, now? This is a society in self-deception and denial. Can it not see, can it really not see, what it is doing?

"Contraceptives" give males all the choices about sex, on the theory that women don't need any choices when this technology is available. But of course it doesn't always work. Then women need "choice." Hence the absolute necessity for access to the utilitarian homicides. The technology of disrespect is corrosive: it corrupts and corrodes every human relationship that it touches.

From the pro-abort rhetoric, you would think that pro-life people are trying to *force* women to become pregnant and bear children. That's called rape, where I come from. But of course the pro-life movement is not impregnating women. It merely asks that women respect the choices that they have already made in their sexual activities, and respect the right to life of their own unborn children. The men who get women pregnant when they don't want to be pregnant (as evidenced by their abortions) are simply invisible in the social ethic of the utilitarian homicides. That ethic was designed to give rampant males complete cover for their actions. It does.

When you ask someone Why?, and keep asking why questions, sooner or later, you stumble into the why-questions that really matter,

## 7.4 Clearings

that tell you what bestows life or imposes death for them. When the questioning comes to a halt at the life issues and someone absolutely has to have access to the utilitarian homicides, you know that his basic life orientation is utilitarian: maximize pleasure, minimize pain. In other words, *not* all of life is good; sometimes exposure, limitation, and need are simply bad, barren, devoid of blessing.

Is there a *reason*, why you "should" embrace all of life as good, including its pains? Something more basic than this choice itself? I don't see that there is; people reason *from* this choice, not *to* it. And people know instinctively that in the question of abortion they are making much larger choices—even if they are males and so not capable of getting pregnant. For a society in which abortion is available will be a very different one from societies that are seriously pro-life.

It is in the pains of life that people choose for or against something much bigger—something that I would call just *life*, life itself. The pains are clearings, places where you can see what people are doing with their lives. If you ask me *why* should we embrace the pains as good, I cannot give you a reason. The most that can be said is that in the end, you will see those who rejected the disappointments of life next to those who embraced them and found blessing in them, sometimes at great cost to themselves. Those who have rejected exposure, limitation, and need can see the comparison, too, and they don't like it; so they won't like you, either, if you choose to look for the blessings in exposure, limitation, and need. When you are faced with the pains of life, when the blessings are not yet apparent, they will say to you, as they said of old, "Israel, where now is your God?"

The God of the Bible is peculiar—different from all other gods, for the other gods promise to deliver the fun parts of life, and they are not there when pain comes. That is why God said to Israel, "You shall have no other gods before me." Pain comes, and God is there, often silent and hidden—but still there. Pain comes, and we pray that, "walking in the way of the cross, we may find it none other than the way of life and peace."

On the Jewish side, the phrasing is a little different; as Joseph Soloveitchik has it, the transcendent God is to be welcomed into the world, not fled to from the world. And that creative halakhic process is one of *tikkun olam*—repairing and completing the blessedness of the created world. Whether Jewish or Christian, the labor of tikkun can become affliction: but the one who chooses to bear the pains of life trusting in life's goodness even when he can't see it knows that he has embraced *life* in its wholeness. In that choice he has forever changed what he is, and this cannot be taken away from him—or her. By anyone.

Whatever happens in civil law about abortion, the issue in biblical (call it covenantal) religion is far more important than merely one more issue in social ethics. For to choose to tolerate abortion within the Covenant is to choose something other than Covenant. What is at stake is nothing less. Covenanters are tempted, just like everybody else; it's not any easier for covenanters or non-covenanters, as statistics attest. To cave in on abortion is to exchange the God who is our glory not for the image of an ox that eats grass (cf. Ps. 106), but for the image of clean surgery getting us out of messy human relationships. To cave in on abortion is to abandon the God of the Bible and convert functionally to polytheism or Gnosticism or nature religions or the Perennial Philosophy. The change is sold in Liberal Theology, of course, under the still-fashionable trademarks of the God of the Bible. A clever marketing strategy, but not truth-in-labeling.

It is never too late to choose life. The man whose woman has had an abortion is in some ways in a worse position than she is, for he has led her into temptation. (The New Testament has harsher words about those who lead others into temptation than about virtually every other sin; something about a millstone, if I recall.) Even he can choose life, if at a terrible cost in rebuilding his own self. Most emphatically, the woman who has had an abortion can still choose life. It is never too late to choose life. Rachel weeps for her lost children, and never weeps more bitterly than when she was abandoned or talked into choosing an

## 7.4 Clearings

abortion against her better judgement. Hard as it is, it is still possible to choose life. Consider the alternatives.

Far from being a digression in this book, the utilitarian homicides represent *the* place where you can see how people today handle exposure, limitation, and need. What began in America in abortion has opened the doorway to the utilitarian homicides that we have seen elsewhere in the twentieth century. Eugenics is back. Abortion leads logically to euthanasia. If it is permissible to terminate lives before birth because someone will suffer exposure, limitation, or need if the child is born alive, why not those who are old, sick, or just medically unattractive? The Holocaust is back, not for Jews, and not in large numbers, but just one or two at a time, for the disabled and the elderly. Whenever a distraught family member murders a disabled person, the lawyers for the defense portray the act as one of "mercy killing." Lawyers will do whatever they have to to get a defendant off. Lawyers have no shame; if repeating the excuses of the Nazis will work (without reminding the jury where those excuses come from), lawyers will cheerfully do that. Much of the public resonates positively to that appeal to pity. But pity is a form of contempt, and "granting them a merciful death" was exactly Hitler's phrase in giving permission for the euthanasia program for the disabled.

We who are disabled have noticed. We remember that the disabled in Germany were the pilot program for the Holocaust, that 85% of all the institutionalized disabled in Germany were killed between 1939 and 1945. (See Burleigh and Gallagher.) They were killed by their doctors, not by the government, the police, the SS, or the National Socialist Party. People today, as then, think they can get away with killing the disabled without it leading to bigger things. If the pains of life bear blessings in a world-affirming basic life orientation, then the fashionable establishment in this society is doing something very un-world-affirming with its life. Abortion and euthanasia are the clearings where you can see that.

## 7.5 That's Too Simple

Why would you want to approach theology the way this book does? Indeed, will this way work?

It works like street signs: it is supposed to tell you where you are in life, and where to go from here. And street signs are supposed to be in street language, ordinary talk. They should not themselves need translations.

If everything is simple in your theory of life, your theory doesn't do justice to life. If everything is complicated, your theory is not user-friendly. Some things should be simple, but you get to choose what is simple because you get to choose where you want to start. Now there are things that are complicated enough in biblical religion. History is the most obvious example, and it can be a tangled story indeed. But even history can be mastered with a little effort. Unraveling a failed engagement with life or a dysfunctional human relationship can be quite complicated. And you can make philosophy—and philosophical theology—as complex and subtle as you like.

But as a practical matter, it is the pains you have to live with. They are the hardest parts to fit into the larger story of your life. If you begin with the pains (they are, after all, what gets your attention first), then everything else should, eventually, fall into place. Theory (here, theology) works best and simplest when it follows practice.

The simple choice of what to do with the pains of life puts people to the question. It is a question that separates basically different ways of living. The language offered here is intended as a way to respect the pains and also to respect the reality that lies behind them, without domesticating that reality.

I think the method here will make most of the perplexities of contemporary theology go away. There have been two main kinds of theology in the twentieth century, and both have problems they cannot solve. The method here solves them easily.

The "conservative" theology, as it is popularly understood, is about

## 7.5 That's Too Simple

"a" being outside the world, one that might or might not exist, a being that interferes with the world to the advantage of those who think it exists and to the disadvantage of those who don't. The sophisticated versions have enough trouble fending off this caricature that there has to be some truth in it. On the other hand, The "conservative" theologies, both Catholic and Protestant, have good enough instincts to handle the life issues—abortion and euthanasia. They know that you can't consistently affirm human life in this world as good without qualification and at the same time end some human lives as not good enough. But their explanations are either uncandid about confessional commitments or else complicated when they should not be, not really what geeks would call "user-friendly."

Liberal Theology long ago decided that it would be better to start with man and the human predicament. In this, I think its instincts are sound. Unfortunately, it never got much beyond human existence. It could worship "faith," but couldn't have faith in much of anything. It never allowed itself anything to sing Te Deum or Non Nobis *to*; its God could never escape being just a figment of human imagination. Lately, Liberal Theology has more serious problems: I think it really doesn't want to embrace all of life as good. Some pains really are unredeemable, and we see that in the way Liberal Theology handles abortion and euthanasia.

Neither variety of theology has done very well with the pains as they come specifically to theology—as history, relativity, and pluralism. (Between the Liberals and the various conservatives lay the Neo-Orthodox among Protestants and a few transcendental Thomists among Catholics. The Neo-Orthodox took critical history seriously, but died without heirs before they could consider its philosophical implications. The Thomists have known all along that God is not a being among other beings, and the Neo-Thomists have begun to think about history. But neither movement is doing much today.)

The "conservatives" have stonewalled modern biblical criticism (the challenge of history), and so have rejected the exposure that comes with it. They have defied religious relativity, instead claiming an absoluteness that simply is not given to creatures. Thus was limitation also rejected. And need is similar; it comes in the form of people of other religions who share a common world and need a common worldview that makes space for them and their traditions. "Conservative" theology orders them to convert or be damned.

The Liberals have no problem with history because they don't care about history—it offers neither risk nor reward. The Liberal approach to cultural relativity and its problems is unconvincing to me, but way too complex to be disentangled here. And plurality is handled with toleration instead of real pluralism: empire ruled by the Liberal Establishment, rather than real community and real respect. Liberal Theology has to retain enough appearance of covenantal promise to pacify at least some of the poor. It is quite ruthless if not at all candid about trashing the weakest and poorest—the unborn and the medically unattractive.

Theology becomes clear if you begin with exposure, limitation, and need, in full confidence that they are the face of encounter with God, and that they bear blessings, bring life and not death. The weaknesses and betrayals of Liberal Theology can be seen easily and corrected. If the "cause" of this blessing-in-disappointment is just left as "The Way Things Are," then there is indeed something to sing *Te Deum Laudamus* to, to sing "Not to us, Lord, but to your name let glory be given." (Psalm 115:1; if you want to sing it, listen to Patrick Doyle's soundtrack for Kenneth Branagh's *Henry V*.) The perplexities of "conservative" theology can't even get started. Exposure, limitation, and need, when embraced, will, eventually, show the way to deal with critical history, cultural relativity and religious pluralism. Unpacking them will be complicated—but the guide to meeting them need not be.

Probably the best reaction to the proposal of this book is, "That's too simple." (But people who complain thus complain not because the starting point is too simple; starting points should always be simple. They complain because they don't like the idea of blessings in the

## 7.5 That's Too Simple

pains of life.) This book may be too *simple*, but it's not too *easy*. There is too much pain in embracing exposure, limitation, and need. Yet a strange thing has happened. Some people have indeed found it to be easy. They have leaped to accept life as good, pains included—and paid with their lives. (But you always pay with your life; it is only a question of what your life will be lived, and spent, for.) The pains can mount to affliction, which is why people *pray* to find the way of the Cross to be the way of life and peace instead of just *declaring* it to be so. They know that they are shooting their mouths off when they promise to embrace exposure, limitation, and need as good-bearing, because they know that this is a promise they don't have the ability to keep—on their own. But if exposure, limitation, and need actually bring their goods within the events themselves, then there is help. Once found, these people never doubted the way, and they rejoiced to say, "that's too easy!"

# For Further Reading

Barbour Ian G., 1997. *Religion and Science; Historical and Contemporary Issues*. San Francisco, HarperSanFrancisco.

Berger, Peter L., and Thomas Luckmann, 1966. *The Social Construction of Reality*. New York: Doubleday.

Berger, Peter L., 1967. *The Sacred Canopy*. New York: Doubleday.

Burleigh, Michael, 1994. *Death and Deliverance: "Euthanasia" in Germany 1900-1945*. New York, Cambridge University Press.

Burrell, David B., 1986. *Knowing the Unknowable God: Ibn-Sina, Maimonides, Aquinas*. University of Notre Dame Press.

Burtt, E. A., 1924. *The Metaphysical Foundations of Modern Physical Science*. Amherst, NY, Humanities Books, 1999. Originally published 1924, 1932, 1952.

Drachmann, A. B., 1922. *Atheism in Pagan Antiquity*. London and Copenhagen: Gyldendal.

Eberstadt, Mary, 2004. "The Family: Discovering the Obvious." *First Things* 140 (2004/02) 10.

Eliade, Mircea, 1949. *The Myth of the Eternal Return; or Cosmos and History*. Princeton: Princeton University Press, 1971. The French original was published in 1949. This book is one of the clearest expositions of the religious differences between nature and history.

Gallagher, Hugh Gregory, 1990. *By Trust Betrayed: patients, physicians, and the license to kill in the Third Reich*. New York: Henry Holt. Gallagher recounts the destruction of the institutionalized disabled in Germany during World War II. It was not done by the government or by the National Socialist Party, but by their doctors. The government merely gave permission. Ironically, Gallagher in recent years seems to countenance the very logic that licensed the German killing. See also Michael Burleigh.

Hertz, Joseph H., 1948; 15th printing, 1974. *The Authorized Daily Prayer Book*, revised edition. New York: Bloch Publishing Company. This is the Siddur, the book of common prayer of rabbinic Judaism. The blessings before the morning Shema are on p. 109.

Hobbs, Edward Craig, 1970. "An Alternate Model from a Theological Perspective." In Herbert A. Otto, *The Family in Search of a Future*. New York: Appleton-Century-Crofts.

Hobbs, Edward Craig, 1973. "Pluralism in the Biblical Context." Berkeley, CA: Pacific Coast Theological Society; http://www.pcts.org/pluralism.html.

Hobbs, Edward Craig, 1974. "Gospel Miracle Story and Modern Miracle Stories," in *Gospel Studies in Honor of Sherman Elbridge Johnson*. Ed. Massey H. Shepherd Jr. and Edward C. Hobbs. *Anglican Theological Review*, Supplemental Series, Number Three, March 1974.

Howell, Patton, PhD, and James Hall, MD, 2002. *Locked in to Life*. Boise, ID: Tea Road Press.

John of Damascus, ca. 600. *An Exact Exposition of the Orthodox Faith*. In *Saint John of Damascus: Writings*. Trans. Frederic H. Chase, Jr. New York: Fathers of the Church, Inc., 1958.

John Paul II, 1984. *Salvifici Doloris*: On the Christian Meaning of Human Suffering. Vatican City, 1984 February 11.

Kenny, Anthony, 1969. *The Five Ways*. London: Routledge and Kegan Paul.

Koyré, Alexandre, 1957. *From the Closed World to the Infinite Universe*. Baltimore: Johns Hopkins University Press.

Lakoff, George, 1987. *Women, Fire, and Dangerous Things; What Categories Reveal about the Mind*. Chicago: University of Chicago Press.

Larson, Gary, *Unnatural Selections*, 1991. Kansas City: Andrews and McNeel. There are many *Far Side* books. Any will do.

Lee, Jung Young, 1996. *The Trinity in Asian Perspective*. Nashville: Abingdon Press.

Lewis, C. S., 1964. *The Discarded Image; An Introduction to Medieval and Renaissance Literature*. Cambridge University Press, 1971.

Littleton, C. Scott, 1982. *The New Comparative Mythology: An Anthropological Assessment of the Theories of Georges Dumézil*, Berkeley and Los Angeles: University of California Press, 3rd ed.

Macquarrie, John, 1966. *Principles of Christian Theology*. New York: Scribners.

McPherson, John, 2000. *Close to Home Uncut*. Kansas City: Andrews and McNeel. Any *Close to Home* books will do.

Mortley, Raoul, 1986. *From Word to Silence*. 2 volumes. Bonn: Hanstein.

Murray, John Courtney, 1964. *The Problem of God*. New Haven: Yale University Press.

Neusner, Jacob, translator, 1984. *The Talmud of Babylonia; An American Translation*. Vol. 1, Tractate Berakhot. Chico: Scholars Press.

Neusner, Jacob, 1988. *The Mishnah: A New Translation*. New Haven: Yale University Press.

Niebuhr, H. Richard, 1960. *Radical Monotheism and Western Culture*. New York: Harper and Row, revised 1970.

Phillips, D. Z. 1986. *Belief, Change and Forms of Life*. Basingstoke: Macmillan. Chapter 4, "The Challenge of What We Know: The Problem of Evil," is directly relevant.

Placher, William C., 1996. *The Domestication of Transcendence: How Modern Thinking About God Went Wrong*. Louisville: Westminster John Knox Press.

Pseudo-Dionysius, ca 500. *Pseudo-Dionysius, The Complete Works*. Trans. Colm Luibheid. New York: Paulist Press, 1987.

Porter, Andrew, and Edward C. Hobbs, 1999. "The Trinity and the Indo-European Tripartite Worldview," *Budhi*, III, nos. 2-3 (1999), pp. 1-28; http://www.jedp.com/trinity.html.

Porter, Andrew, 2001. *By The Waters of Naturalism: Theology Perplexed Among the Sciences*. Eugene, Oregon: Wipf and Stock Publishers.

Rocca, Gregory, OP, 1993. "Aquinas on God-Talk: Hovering Over the Abyss." *Theological Studies* 54 (1993) 641.

Brian K. Smith, 1994. *Classifying the Universe: The Ancient Varna System and the Origins of Caste.* New York: Oxford University Press. This is a good source for more recent work on Dumézil's tripartition thesis.

Soloveitchik, Joseph, 1983. *Halakhic Man.* Translated by Lawrence Kaplan. Philadelphia: Jewish Publication Society, 1983. Originally published as "Ish ha-halakhah" in *Talpiot* I, nos. 3–4 (New York, 1944).

Thomas Aquinas, ca 1273. *In quatros libros sententiarum Magistri Petri Lombardi.* In Volume 6 of the Opera Omnia. Parma, 1856. Reprinted, New York: 1948. There are other editions.

Westphal, Merold, 1984. *God, Guilt and Death; An Existential Phenomenology of Religion.* Bloomington: Indiana University Press. The last three chapters are the application to our problems.

# Index

analogy, 42, 43, 46, 51, 70–74, 93, 94, 98, 105, 106, 114, 119, 120
Anselm, vii
Aristotle, 63, 64, 69, 90
Avicenna, 86

Barth, Karl, 5
beatific vision, 89, 127
Berger, Peter L., 118, 122
Beutner, Edward, 127
bloids, 69
Buddhism, 102, 103, 109
Bultmann, Rudolf, 85
Burleigh, Michael, 135
Burrell, David B., 64
Burtt, E. A., 112

Calvin, John, 85
Calvinists, 54
Camus, Albert, 23, 24, 34, 38
Close to Home, 58
confessional commitment, 38, 41, 120–122, 137
Constitution, U. S., 32
creation, 6, 10, 21, 33, 75, 97

creaturehood, 2, 19, 21, 58, 59, 69, 98, 115, 138
Deuteronomic Sermon, vii, 39, 77, 111
Documents, Common, definition of, 10
Dumézil, Georges, 29, 30, 103

Eliade, Mircea, 65, 95
Exodus 3.14, the burning bush, 6, 47, 50, 53, 55, 80, 86, 87, 89
Exodus, the, 4, 9, 36, 47, 54, 56, 72, 88, 89, 96, 101

faith, distributed ontology of, 128
Far Side, The, 19, 57–59
Feuerbach, Ludwig, 104
Freud, Sigmund, 104

Gallagher, Hugh Gregory, 135
Gnosticism, 6, 60, 76, 134
God, existence of, vii, 42, 56, 60, 62, 81–85, 87, 119
God, interfering, 51, 56, 59, 60, 93, 113, 137

God, named as Nothing, 69, 80, 81, 89, 120, 121, 127
God, named as Void, 55, 80, 85
God, simplicity of, 64

heavenly banquet, 127
Heidegger, Martin, 68, 84, 85
Hellenistic world, 29, 31, 52, 53, 100
Hobbs, Edward, 3, 4, 13, 14, 21, 33, 68, 115
Holocaust, 135

I Ching, the, 109
Indo-European tripartite ideology, 27–30, 32, 33, 35, 36, 100–103, 105–109
Isaiah, 2, 7–9, 14, 42, 54, 92, 120, 128

Jesus, 7, 14–17, 27, 36, 54, 69, 80, 101, 102, 106, 108, 114, 115, 128
Job, 8
John of Damascus, 84, 86
John Paul II, viii
Joshua, vii, 39, 56, 57, 77, 98, 111

Kenny, Anthony, 62–64
Kierkegaard, Søren, 121
Koyré, Alexandre, 112

Lakoff, George, 106

Lao Tzu, 109, 110
Larson, Gary, 57
Lee, Jung Young, 109
Leibniz, G. W., 5, 117
Lewis, C. S., 70–73, 113
Liberal Theology, 129, 134, 137, 138
logical positivism, 72
Lutherans, 54

Macquarrie, John, 84
Mallory, George Leigh, 37
Mason, David, 24
miracles, 3, 4, 15–17, 24, 102, 114, 115
monotheism, radical, 6, 10, 14, 54, 56, 69, 103, 119, 121
Monty Python, 16, 46, 72
Moore, Ethan, 118
Morgan, Donn, 3
Mortley, Raoul, 83
Moses, 6, 47, 50, 53, 55, 86, 89, 96
Murphy, John Michael, 81
Murray, John Courtney, 50, 51, 86, 89

naturalism, 3, 46, 60, 61, 75, 95, 111, 112
nature, order in, 34, 61, 95–97, 101
Neoplatonism, 45, 76, 83, 85
Niebuhr, H. Richard, 54–56, 85

Nixon, Richard, 32

pantheism, 41, 45, 75
Perennial Philosophy, 76, 134
Phillips, D. Z., viii, 119, 120
Philo of Alexandria, 27, 107–109
Placher, William, 60, 64, 65, 84
Plato, 27, 71, 73, 83
Platonism, 56, 57, 60, 63, 71–73, 75
polytheism, 69, 134
Porter, Andrew, 33
Prometheus, 18
Propp, William, 47
prosopon, 22, 28, 81
Pseudo-Dionysius, 83–87, 89

rabbis, 8, 9, 36, 54, 106
religion, covenantal, 7, 14, 18, 57, 88, 90, 127, 134
religion, Indo-European, 30–33, 100
religion, world-affirming, historical, 9, 58, 96, 114–116, 119, 135
religion, world-affirming, nature, 10, 33, 34, 58, 59, 95, 96, 101, 114, 134
Rocca, Gregory, OP, 85–87, 89
Romans, epistle to, 5, 8, 9, 14
Russell, Bertrand, 54, 55

Salvifici Doloris, viii, 121
Sartre, Jean-Paul, 122
Sayers, Dorothy, 43
Shema, the, 8, 9, 106
Sirica, John, 32
sociodicy, 118
Soloveitchik, Joseph, 109, 134
Supreme Court of the United States, 131

Talmud, 8, 9, 82
Tao Te Ching, 109, 110
Tao, the, 110
Taoism, 106, 110
Temple in Jerusalem, 36, 52–54
The Way Things Are, as name of God, 41–46, 74–78, 93
theodicy, viii, 117–122
Thomas Aquinas, 62–66, 69, 84–87, 89, 90
tikkun olam, 108, 109, 134
Tillich, Paul, 84
transcendence, 10, 45–47, 57–61, 64, 70–75, 84, 110, 127, 134
transcendence, domesticated, 45, 60, 64, 70, 73, 75, 136
Trinity, 13–23, 28–30, 33, 35, 36, 103, 105, 109
Troeltsch, Ernst, 3, 4, 114

unanswerable questions, 59, 61, 62, 65–68, 70, 73, 75, 82

Voltaire, 5
Vonnegut, Kurt, 43

Weitsman, Jonathan, 8

xscreensaver, 104

www.ingramcontent.com/pod-product-compliance
Lightning Source LLC
Chambersburg PA
CBHW070907160426
43193CB00011B/1395